# LIFE WITHOUT SOCKS

# LIFE WITHOUT SOCKS

## VIEWS FROM A BARMAID

By Carole Paulson

One
InTen
PUBLISHING
COMPANY

This is a work of fiction. Names, places and incidents are products of the author's imagination or are used fictitiously. Any resemblance to actual persons, living or dead, is entirely coincidental.

Cover design by Skot O'Mahony

First Edition
Printed in the United States of America
ISBN# 0-9628479-0-9

One In Ten Publishing has offices at
1135 11th Avenue, Suite 200, Seattle, Washington 98122

*ঔ৳৹*

There are so many of you who have made my life what it is and so many of you who have given me the material for this book. You all know who you are, and—hopefully—you know your code names as well. If I try to name you all, being the blonde I am, I will inevitably end up leaving someone out and run the risk of being talked about behind my back, so I respectfully decline to name drop at this point.

I do however wish to make one exception: David Kenobbie, you are a stubborn shit. I love you. Hang in there and beat this thing, or I promise the next time, I tell all your secrets!!

"If I could have anything? I'd ask for the moon."

*Note:* David Kennobie, like so many others, has gone. He is loved. He is missed.

*ঔ৳৹*

5

# PREFACE

I have always read that the pen is mightier than the sword and that humor is universal. I have also read that people from outer space built the Great Pyramids and that Bigfoot is in fact Oscar Wilde's jilted lover, doomed to roam the Earth until someone finds out who really killed J.F.K. It just goes to show you that you can only believe half of what you read.

In writing this book I kept in mind that it is important for all of us to find the courage to laugh at ourselves. Life, taken too seriously, runs the risk of turning us all into Eggplants and if you've ever tried to be an Eggplant for any length of time you know how dull it can be.

"Celebrate the Differences" sounds like such a corny phrase but you get the drift, and it's pretty to the point.

One more thing. There has been a lot of speculation as to who really wrote this book, whether it was me or, in fact, Breaker Morant—the big white cat who graciously allows me to live with him. Let me clear the whole thing up for once and for all: If you love the book, I wrote it. If you hate the book, please address all hate mail to Breaker Morant, c/o of the publisher.

Sincerely,
The Barmaid (and her cat)

# LIFE WITHOUT SOCKS
## Another Coming Out Story

A couple of Friday nights ago while I was cocktailing, I met yet another twenty-one year old gay person. This twenty-one year old was a very handsome young man but he was troubled. His dark brooding eyes were made darker by his pensive attitude and his naturally rebellious locks were forced into calm ringlets by his depression. I bought him a drink—someone had to do it—and asked if I could get him anything else. "Yeah," he answered sarcastically, "how about a new set of parents."

"You're not having fun with the old ones?" I shouted above the blare of the video.

"Kind of like that," he replied. "See, I just came out, and I don't think they're going to take it well at all."

"Do you have to tell them?" I asked. That is always my first question since I know over a third of my friends have never really taken that step.

"I feel I do," he pouted. "I just think they are going to explode."

"Well," I said sympathetically, "I'm not the best in the advice department, but I do remember telling my parents, and I do remember strange situations from friends who haven't told theirs so maybe I can help."

He downed his drink and laughed bitterly, "Sure, you can have me over for Christmas and Thanksgiving from now on—after I tell them."

"What makes you think they're going to disown you?"

"Well," he said, "They're pretty religious, and gay is not smiled upon by the higher being."

I smiled at this guy, now he was in my territory and I did have a story to share with him. I lit a cigarette, and with this young man in tow,

I began a journey down one of the foot-trails along memory lane..."let me tell you about LIFE WITHOUT SOCKS."

I was eighteen when I first realized that perhaps I was following the beat of a different drummer so to speak. I didn't look like I was headed that way. On the contrary, I looked the way I had been raised: very feminine, very straight, and very Mormon. My parents had raised me for the sole purpose of getting married and replenishing the earth. Hopefully I would at least sort of like the other half of my replenishing partnership, but I don't think, given the possible alternatives, that this was their prime concern. I was in my first month of my first year of college and was taking a drama class, ("Draem-ah" as my mother always managed to pronounce it) when I came face to face with my unravelling. Her name was Lyn. I've always suspected the name Lyn, spelled L-Y-N meant something along the lines of 'loss of control' or 'parents' enemy' or 'your daughter is one', something like that, something that warns you a great change is about to take place, one our parents didn't foresee, one they didn't tell you about when you were fourteen and sitting in the back row of health class located in the basement of the school gymnasium. My Lyn was in the form of a very beautiful, very androgynous woman just a shade older than myself. I found the shade to be intriguing—in truth, I found everything about her to be intriguing.

Intriguing? My, how subtle I've hoped to become in my older years. Actually I wanted her in the worst way and if that was standing up in a hammock—so be it. Perhaps I wouldn't have chased her so mercilessly if I hadn't believed her to be a card carrying lesbian, but I was young then and didn't realize that androgyny was not necessarily a prerequisite for lesbianism. No, in my mind she was a definite lesbian...and she wanted me.

I followed her everywhere she went, did everything she did and made subtle suggestions every chance I got. My friend "Mikey" suggested I hang a sign around my neck that said "Take Me", he made some other suggestions too that don't bear repeating. Finally it happened. Lyn invited me to her house for the weekend. That was all I needed. I, who had always been the responsible daughter and child did not even remember to tell my parents that I had gone, I just went and it was magic.

Perhaps I should have gone home after the weekend—after all, I was still living with mom and dad. Perhaps Lyn and I shouldn't have walked all over campus arm in arm, hand in hand, heads bent. I'm sure I'd do it all different now, but back then all I knew was that something magical had happened, something I had secretly waited for since I had heard my first fairy tale.

They called me at Lyn's on Tuesday night. I hadn't been home since Friday. My mother had heard something from my best friend about my behavior on campus. Not her little girl!!! They asked me to come home for a family conference, she begged me to be "okay." Sick with dread I took a bus to the east side where I lived, where they lived, where we once had lived together.

When I got inside the house there was no one at home besides my brother.

"Baseball," I said, "I think I love a woman."

"Great!" he said and went back to sniffing glue. I saw the dog.

"Brut," I said, "I think I love a woman."

He looked at me, yawned, and went back to licking his penis. This was not helping me prepare for the mom and dad, not in the least. I told the fireplace, the rhododendron bush, the silver tea service and the new patchwork print couch and chair which clashed with the rest of the living room. Nothing moved, changed color or disintegrated— I knew it would be different when mom and dad got there.

At six forty-two they entered the house. "Are you a lesbian?" my dad asked shakily.

"What's a lesbian?" I countered.

"A woman who loves women," he replied.

"Well, then no," I reasoned, "because I only love one woman."

That's when my mom ran out of the room screaming and called every relative she remembered. I could hear her in the back bedroom wailing Irish curses and announcing the news while my dad tried to reason with me. Finally after fall turned to winter (or so it seemed) my mother came out of the bedroom. She leveled her gaze on me and with much composure said, "Barmaid, I just cannot accept this...this...'phase' you are going through. Going through life without a man, is like going through life without socks. It's just not dignified."

I waited for more flash, more fireworks, but that was all. The conversation was finished. I moved out of the house that night and for the next year pondered many things. I missed my parents and was devastated that they didn't understand, but at the same time I was proud of myself for being honest with them. We had always had

11

honesty between us and at least that hadn't changed.

That first Christmas was very hard, for them too I'm sure, but somehow I made it through and then, right before my birthday something wonderful happened..I received a letter in the mail—actually it was more like clippings with a note attached.. The note read:

"As you can see from these clippings, I guess I may have been a bit hasty. It appears that going sock-less is now in fashion, I love you, please come home to dinner for your birthday and bring your friend, love, Mom."

The pictures were of new spring fashions—short pants, Keds and yes, no socks.

It's been almost 10 years since then, and my parents have been two of my best friends. They don't always understand, but I don't always understand either, "life without socks" isn't always easy.

"Great story," the guy said as he stood up to leave; he walked toward the bathroom and it occurred to me that you probably had to be there. Later that night however, after the bar had closed and only the employees were left, the janitor came out of the men's bathroom looking ever so perplexed.

"What a weird night," he said, "Look, some guy left these in the john." While others crowded around to identify the pieces held by the dumbfounded janitor, I just stayed in my place and smiled. I knew what the janitor had found because I had seen the young man when he left the bar, and he was showing a well turned ankle.

# GAY LIKE ME

## Or The Days Of Whine & Moses

The phrase 'Coming out' is not akin to 'coming in' or 'going out.' 'Coming in' for instance, clearly suggests entering a place, while 'going out' suggests leaving. 'Coming out,' on the other hand, is neither entering or leaving but rather the revolving door effect. I was privileged enough to experience my 'Coming out' companion, my best friend since high school, a 19 year old gay man I shall call 'Mikey'.

Mikey and I had done everything together since we were fifteen, so it came as no surprise that we decided that we were gay together. We had each had our respective "first experience" and had decided simultaneously that this new-found sexuality was right for us. Unfortunately our prospects had also simultaneously flown the coop, so to speak. It was most devastating. You see, realizing you are gay at nineteen presents some pretty serious difficulties. With a face like the Campbell soups kids you can't expect to get into a gay bar....and we were quick to realize that gay people didn't exactly frequent Bellevue wearing sandwich boards proclaiming their sexuality. As a matter of fact, the harder we looked, the more it seemed that everyone on earth was planning to get married and have children. We had just about decided to give up the whole idea of ever finding those elusive beings referred to as "Gay" when-poof! In walked 'Whine' and 'Moses'.

We were at a movie (*La Cage Aux Folles*) and we had just come to the conclusion that all gay people lived in France, when I felt a hot stare penetrating me from the middle of the darkened movie isle. I looked up and saw the smokey eyes of the Bellevue Cinema usherette staring at me unabashedly. I quickly took my feet off of the seat in front of me, assuming that once again I was in trouble for bad movie manners. She smiled slowly and shook her head no. In case I missed her meaning she leaned over and whispered low and throaty, "You're not in trouble with me...." then she was gone. A few minutes later a rather good looking boy, in a flowing scarf, sat himself next to Mikey and said, "My friend, the usherette, she likes your friend, the blond." Mikey looked at the boy in the scarf, and then I felt him dig a large groove into my shin with the heel of his new Brahma Bull cowboy boots. I tried not to scream, but my only other involuntary response would have been to beat the bloody pulp out of him, so I opted for my first choice. The boy, who thought I had been offended by his whispered information, lithely removed himself from the seat and was gone—just like the usherette!!

"Well, you really blew that!!" announced Mikey in a voice so loud that half the theater turned to ask *what* I had blown. I myself was more concerned about where these mysterious people were slipping off to. Was there a trap door underneath our seats or what??

"C'mon, lets get out of here before I seriously embarrass myself," he whispered while looking around at the still-curious audience. We made our way to the lobby just as our new-found friends had decided to re-enter the darkened theatre. The four of us ended up in a helter-skelter pile-up reminiscent of "how many people can *you* fit in a phone booth?"

"Well," said the throaty usherette, "I think introductions are in order."

"Me too," I agreed hastily trying to remove my hand from the usherette's breast area. My nineteen-year old knee had precociously lodged itself in her crotch during the fall, and I knew my face would never be any color but red again.

"This is 'Whine', and I'm 'Moses' " she informed us gaily, "And we were thinking the two of you might like some company." Mikey and I smiled at each other.

"This only happens in the movies!" he whispered to me, but no it was real life and it was really happening.

As time went on we found out lots about 'Whine' and 'Moses'. They were only nineteen just like us but their difference in knowledge was vast. They were truly gay—knew all about it!!! Mikey and I emulated their every trait, and they were more than willing to be our mentors.

'Whine' taught Mikey how to talk in a high pitched voice, how to hold his cigarette and how all gay men wear flowing scarfs. Mikey was so thankful. He would have never known all of those things "real" gay

14

men do if he hadn't met someone like 'Whine'. Geez, he probably would have gone to his first gay bar dressing and acting like a nerd!! The same went for me. I didn't know that all lesbians cut their hair two inches short all over and that women was spelled with a 'y'. That the color pink was developed by chauvinist male pigs to oppress weak womyn and that God, Buddha, Jesus, Moses, Henry the Eighth and Oral Roberts were all secretly womyn.

Finally, through our mentors, we had learned all of the things that *real* gay people know. It was now time for the test...The "Coming out" party!!! We were finally going to our first gay bar!!!

Mikey and I were so excited we could hardly contain ourselves. In the rush to get there Mikey had almost forgotten his flowing scarf. I, however, could never forget my new lesbian haircut as it was scathingly short—two inches all over. We entered our first gay bar knowing we were the height of gay fashion when suddenly my eyes accustomed to light. "Jesus Mikey, don't look!" I screamed.

"Why? What's wrong!!??!" he screamed back. Just then I saw Mikey's face fall to the floor. The men there weren't wearing flowing scarfs; they didn't talk in high-pitched voices or smoke like Bette Davis...they were just regular guys the same as Mikey before he had met "Whine"!! The same went for me. That night, I heard more Lesbian women use the word 'gal' than I thought possible. A lot of them had long hair too, and no one I met thought that Oral Roberts was a woman.

Two months later 'Moses' shipped off for Alaska and 'Whine' and Mikey broke it off. Mikey had met another man, one who wore muscle shirts and smoked Marlboros—not that it mattered to Mikey. He had learned his lesson about being yourself. I, eventually got involved with a woman who drove a motorcycle—of course I bought one myself—it still sits in the garage. You see, I don't know how to drive it yet, but so what??? It's not that I think every "Dyke" should have one...that's too stereotypical—it's just that I believe...well I believe...ummmm...that no woman should be without one!!! Yea!! That's it!!

# 𝔸 SEPARATE PEACE

It was probably around the second year of my being gay that I heard the term "separatist."

It was used very vaguely at a youth meeting, but somehow I understood it to be linked with "politically correct." At the time in my life, having no idea what "politically correct" meant, but knowing I must be that at all costs, I decided to embark on a life of "separatism."

Unfortunately, I had no idea what "separatism" meant.

I decided to ask my lesbian mentor, 'Moses', to explain. That of course , was my first mistake. You see, Moses has always been fairly black-and-white about everything, so in explaining separatism she said simply, "One who separates him or herself from the mainstream. In your case, separating would mean cutting yourself off from any contact with the heterosexual community."

That was all I needed to hear. I've always been a purist in every sense of the word, and when I commit to something, I commit whole heartedly. Hence, I embarked on my separate journey.

I was living on Capital Hill in Seattle at the time. I was in a small downstairs apartment on Federal Ave. E. The apartment was in very poor condition, and I hated to be in it; on the first day of my separatism, however, I felt I had to get my priorities in order, and so I decided to spend the day at home. The first thing I did that morning was quit my job. Well, the business was owned by straight people, and since I must "cut myself off from the heterosexual community," I couldn't very well waltz into work and begin to fold sheets like nothing had happened! No indeed! I was on a crusade!

I decided that crusading made me very hungry, so after I hung up the phone I decided to make some breakfast. But wait! Where did these eggs come from?? And this bacon? Did the farmers who owned these animals respect gay rights? Did the truckers who delivered these

17

products have gay friends ? What about the road builders?

I was on a roll, and there was no stopping me now. What about the workers who built my oven? The fry pan? The silverware? Suddenly it dawned on me. I couldn't eat. Not this food. It wasn't gay food.

Well, I just have to go without until I could find some gay food. Hmmm. I decided to watch T.V. No, I couldn't. There weren't any gay T.V. shows on and I didn't know the first thing about the company who made my set. They might be homophobic ass holes. Reading was a better choice.

I went to my bookshelves and began to toss out book after book. I had never realized how many non-gay authors I had collected over the years. Poe wasn't gay; neither was Dickens. I could keep Oscar Wilde, Plato, Stein, and my copy of *Rubyfruit Jungle*. Being politically correct was getting tough.

I decided to take a bath and relax. I was running the water, had one foot in the tub when I was struck by another bolt of lightning—who made my bathtub? Was I just about to step into a porcelain vessel of uneducated prejudice?

Not me! Not this Barmaid. Oh no, I was determined to be the epitome of separatism. I was slightly bugged that at this point I couldn't eat, bathe, watch T.V. or read a book, but I was committed to the cause, by golly. (Well, maybe not by golly.)

I needed a nap. I approached my warm little bed and —yep, you guessed it—turned and ran out of the apartment. None of the stuff in there was "for sure." I didn't know who made any of the things I owned and used, from the band-aids in the bathroom to the zither in my bedroom closet.

My life was a shambles. I got in my car probably made by queer bashers and drove down the public roads (I never noticed how straight they were laid before) to the nearest lesbian bar. (I wondered who originally built that bar.) At least in the company of other women maybe my poor head would quit aching.

I entered the dark, empty bar, and with my probably straight-tailored clothes just dripping, sat on a bar stool of unknown origin. I ordered a beer. It was a draught (served in a glass from who knows where). I realized how depressing it was not knowing anything about the daily necessities of your life.

The bartender must of been reading my mind because she leaned over the oak bar and whispered " Got a problem?"

"A big one," I answered.

"Anything you want to talk about?"

For me, those were the magic words. I poured out the details in a non-stop rush until, exhausted, I had to take a pause.

"A separatist, huh?" She grinned. "A separatist purist Lesbian, with no home, no food and no car. You can't even be sure about those clothes, you know. In order to follow your high ideals you're going to have to find some pretty dense woods and start from scratch."

"Look," I said, almost crying, "It may be funny to you, but I'm trying to make a change in the world—in the way things are. Being a separatist is making a statement!!"

She looked at me hard.

"Barmaid, you are a writer, and you have a pretty good sense of humor; in the long run you're going to make a much bigger, broader statement by reaching out than by running off. Besides, if you insist on being a purist separatist, then I'm going to do my part by not letting you out of this bar with those clothes on, as I doubt you know whether or not inspector #55 is gay. Think about it—it's a long, naked walk from here to the woods."

I learned a lesson that day. Not from anything the Bartender said, but more from the pile of books on the floor that greeted me on my return home.

What if *they* had all been separatists? What if they had never written because they didn't know where the paper had come from, where the ink was made, who printed the books? What if they had lived in the woods and never met the characters who inspired them? The people they loved, the people they hated, the wrongs they saw committed and the written words they composed to remind people throughout time that communication is the beginning of understanding?

All these things went through my head simultaneously, and I realized the Bartender was right. I smiled to myself then. I had only one regret; I wished I'd come to that realization before I'd left the bar... naked.

# A GENTLE CURE-ALL FOR GENDER HATRED

In this age of community togetherness, love, goodwill, and the push for peace, it probably isn't too posh to talk about segregation.

I don't mean racial segregation or even religious segregation. The segregation I refer to is less popular and far more subtle. While it does happen on a world-wide level, it is interesting to note that in such a permissive subculture as ours, we also find ourselves guilty at times of the same segregation, the same prejudice if you will—the type of prejudice known as "gender hating."

Years ago, in the gay community it was a common occurrence to see all-female gay bars and all-male gay bars. Not many people thought anything about it. After all, men were men, and they did "men's things," and women were women and needed bigger bathrooms.

Then a few years ago things started changing. Gay men and women realized that perhaps they weren't so different. They both wanted the same civil rights. Why, a lot of them drank the same drink! Suddenly it was possible that gay men and women could co-exist—not only in the same community, not only in the same neighborhood, but in the same gay bars as well!

Happy days were here again! At this point almost everyone jumped on the bandwagon and became what we refer to as "united". This story, however, is not about those folks.

Perhaps the bandwagon had a full load. Perhaps a few hapless souls missed the pick-up point. Whatever happened, needless to say, some old die-hards made it under a rock and re-emerged later still hating the opposite sex.

This story is about them. And you. And my dog.

21

I was fortunate enough to work at a gay men's bar a few years ago and at the time just happened to be the only female cocktail waitress there.  It was during this time that I met my first "woman hater."

Now "hate" is a pretty strong word, and —although I hesitate to use it—when I served this man a drink, he yelled at the bartender, "If I wanted to be served by a crack, I'd go to a dyke bar!"  I hesitate more to use the word *dislike*.  Even though the management (gay males all) informed him he could be polite or drink elsewhere, I now knew the score.

What a strange feeling to be hated for what you were, what you couldn't change.  Why, it was almost like —like being gay!

Hey, wait a minute!  I was being hated for what I was by a guy who *knew* what it was like to be hated for what he was!  This made no sense.  I decided to win him over no matter how hard it would be.

His name was Michael, and for months he made my life miserable because, inadvertently, I made his life miserable.  Here we were, just the two of us miserable together night after night in this bar.  I'd talk to him; he'd ignore me.  He'd scowl at me.  I'd ignore the scowl.

I was about ready to give up when, lo and behold, up popped Valentine's Day.

Now, I get a real kick out of Valentine's Day even though Valentine's Day doesn't feel the same way about me.  I never seem to have a lover on Valentine's Day.  I guess it's just an unlucky day for me. (Once I had a lover up until the day before.  That's the closest I've come.)

Apparently it was the same for Michael.  For here we were, just the two of us, together on "lovers day".  I got off work early (there was no one in the bar besides Michael), and so, without thinking, I sat down right next to him.

"Well, another *fabulous* V. Day!" I sarcastically said to no one in particular.

"No kidding," a voice next to me grunted.

Wait a minute.  This wasn't just any voice.  This was the voice of Michael the Scowler.  I became very excited inside but acted nonchalant so as not to let him realize the crime he had committed.

"You know," I sighed (again to no one in particular—ha, ha). "I've never had a lover on Valentine's Day."

"So," he said. (Pick *my* face up off the floor.) "I've never even gotten a Valentine."

"Not even in school?!" I exclaimed. "I thought it was a mandatory rule to get at least one Valentine in school."

"No. Actually, I was pretty homely as a kid."

This was hard to believe, as he was fairly attractive now, and I told him so.

"You think so," he said, and actually turned to face me.

"Well, as men go," I quickly recovered. I didn't want to give too much all at once.

"Well, the guys must not see what you see because I sure haven't had much luck there lately."

"It must run in cycles, " I said, "Because I'm not doing well, either."

"Well, screw it anyway," he snorted and turned back to his drink.

Just then I remembered something. I waved to the bartender subtly to get Michael a drink on me and then excused myself to go to the bathroom. In my coat I remembered a Valentine I had purchased to send to my mom. I got it out and wrote a little poem, signed and sealed it and on the front of the envelope in a trembling hand wrote "Michael." I came back into the bar and when he wasn't looking, I slipped it under his drink, then disappeared for a few minutes.

When I came back, he was smiling. At me!

"I've given you a pretty hard time, haven't I?" he asked.

"No problem," I smiled back. "Why don't we go see what else is happening in this town tonight?"

"Are you buying?" he laughed.

The evening was actually pretty fun. We went to several men's bars where Michael's reputation changed drastically. He found that I was a great conversation piece. More men asked him what he was doing out with a woman after the fuss he'd made than had talked to him all year.

The only mishap during the evening was down at the local girl's bar, when a very large woman of lesbian descent shouldered up to him and growled, "You know, I really hate pricks." He and I had a pretty good laugh over that.

To this day, Michael is a dear friend of mine, and while I'm sure he's received many other Valentine's cards since then, mine still sits above his mantle, complete with the little poem I wrote inside:

Roses are red
I don't give a damn
If I had a weenie
Then I'd be a man!

23

One more thing, I said this article was also about my dog. Well, when Michael took me home that night, he stopped in my apartment to have a nightcap.

He never got one. He had to leave because my dog kept trying to bite him.

I don't know what gets into that dog, but sometimes he just hates men.

# WHEN IN ROME...

Travel. The word sends shivers of excitement down our spines. It brings to mind scenes of luxurious vacations, new places, friendly faces... strange cultures and customs born from centuries of tradition, rooted in the hearts of a proud people. Travel broadens our minds and enriches our field of experience and when we grow old our mental snapshots keep the world bright. Yes, travel brings to mind all these things and more, until you've had your first VACATION FROM HELL!!

Vacations from Hell are not made, they are born. True to form, a vacation always has at least one of two accomplices. The place you go, and the people you go with. For my vacation, I somehow ended up with both. I probably should have sensed the warning signs the minute they came up, but I was tired and really needed to get away. I had been to San Francisco before, (or so I had thought) and the idea of taking a trip with my three closest partners in crime seemed like a lot of fun. At that time in my life, I had never had the pleasure of doing something that was too much fun. You know, the kind of fun that almost kills you. Each time I had gone to San Francisco before it was a trip involving museums, art and culture among friends. I should have known that with PicNic, Rambo and Stretch this trip would basically involve bars, bars and more bars.

The flight down was enough to convince me to jump on the next flight back. Rambo terrorized the whole crew in less than two hours. I'm sure that Lybia would pay dearly for a man with his talents. His lover and my dear friend PicNic tried to calm him down and when that failed just figured it was best to join him. What a great idea!!

The two of them disembarked completely inebriated due to the fact that Rambo had figured out how to get as many cocktails as he wanted during the flight. He deduced that if he went around the plane and asked every person who wasn't drinking to order a bottle of Cutty Sark and offered them an extra dollar to do so, he'd have enough drinks for the flight. The stewards claimed they had never in the history of that run gone through so many bottles of Cutty Sark.

We were somehow able to escape without being incarcerated. I personally believe that the airline just did not want to take the responsibility for holding us there until the authorities arrived. Whatever the reason, we made our way out of the airport, some of us weaving and some of us leading the weavers, to find the friend who was to pick us up.

I was excited. Our friend, Mellow, was a calm sort of man and I knew he would change the tone of our already out-of-control vacation. I had met him two or three times when he had come up to Washington and I had ultimate faith. Bad idea. Mellow met us wearing a pair of neon Bermuda shorts that said, "Let's Party!" across the crotch area. This normally conservative man had gone all out for his vacationers, even donning a Rainier beer drinking cap. I wanted to pretend that we did not know the man but unfortunately he was standing up and waving to us from inside his 1960 Buick convertible, one foot on the horn, of course. I dashed to the car totally mortified. The last time I could remember being that embarrassed was back in Junior High when my Dad drove me to the Christmas dance in our old beat up '57 Fairlane and my best friend recognized my new Christmas dress to be made of none other than our old living room draperies. As Stretch and the boys mamboed their way to the car I realized that this was going to be a page out of my most embarrassing moments book. "Well, thank God that's over," I said under my breath as the group piled into the car. Now we'd be going to our motel, a hopefully quite place called Beck's Motor Lodge, where I could relax and my peers could sleep it off. Maybe a little later we could all head out to the museum, I was thinking pleasantly when it dawned on me that the car was heading away from town.

"Hey Guy's, Where are we going!?" I yelled over the wind. No one answered me because they were all too busy practicing simultaneous hand signals/gay waves.

"I'm serious!" I screamed. "Where are we headed?"

"Sausalito!" the rest of the group yelled in unison. Where had I been? Of course we had all decided to go to Sausalito! Silly me! I bet we had all decided to get more drinks as well! How special!!! Sure enough, minutes later we were double parking right in front of the

Sausalito Inn, a notoriously Gay hangout and surprise surprise, drinking establishment. Four cocktails and twenty minutes later, we were on the road again. We had been 86'd for double parking. Next stop, the Lyon Pub. At this quaint little stop, our group from Seattle taught their group to drink "Blow Jobs" (of course the whole bar round was compliments of Rambo) and we were making friends right and left. Unfortunately somebody's lover felt that Rambo was just a bit too friendly and because that somebody was the bartender, we put in our prompted resignation at the Lyon Pub. On to the Cafe San Marcos, which was a men's bar until we got through with it. It has always been my suspicion that since the night of PicNic, Rambo and Mellow, men just became too afraid to come in there again and so it became a women's hangout. We also left there under suspicious circumstances.

Not letting any grass grow under our feet we made our way to the Elephant Walk, which has since burned down. Things were getting pretty wild and I was forced to start drinking beer just to take the edge off of reality. I decided there must be a form of rescue somewhere out there in this big city and so, as a last resort, I called my friend Saint and asked her to meet us at our next stop which was a place called The Twin Peaks. Saint arrived with her friend, a semi conservative woman I shall call Scott Scott. Finally relief! PicNic decided he needed to be wearing some leather and so disappeared to change leaving Rambo in the bar by himself. Bad Mistake. Anticipating some disaster, I talked the girls into sitting with me quietly on the upper level where we could keep a bird's-eye view on Rambo without being a direct part of his tomfoolery. Rambo did not think this was very funny. He motioned to us several times to come down and join him as he once again was playing student teacher to a new group of "Blow Job" drinkers but we politely declined with a group turn of our heads. This only served to make him more adamant. We ignored him. Wrong move. He decided that we could not possibly ignore him if he dropped his pants in the middle of the bar and gave a big B.A. in our direction. The idea was well formed but something went very wrong in the execution. Rambo dropped his Levis and took a deep bend intending to put his head between his legs in order to see our shocked faces. He put his head further between his legs straining to find us up on the loft but we weren't there, not with the whole bar looking up to see what fools Rambo, the party maniac, was mooning. What happened next was totally unexpected, the bartender, seeing some asshole (literally) acting up in his bar, jumped over the counter and began pushing Rambo out of the bar onto the street. Rambo, panic-stricken went to lift his head up so that he could explain but alas, his head became stuck in his pants and he could not pull it free. Out into the street went his B.A. and the rest of him as well just in time to be seen by a furious Leather PicNic. PicNic had wisely driven the convertible up to the bar intending to give us a ride to our next destination. Out of the car he jumped and shoved Rambo's bare ass into the back seat. Rambo was not able to right himself and looked rather like an Ostrich or a dwarf Cyclops depending on which angle you viewed him from.

"Come one, Girls, we're leaving" PicNic yelled into the bar. Saint and Scott Scott looked at each other and said they would prefer to follow us in their own car. Needless to say, we never saw them again. By this time, I myself am feeling no pain due to the beers and since San Francisco is such a friendly town, I suggest that we find a mixed bar and go dancing.

The thing I like about San Francisco," I say confidently, "is the way that we all are welcome in any bar. It's like there is no prejudice, no segregation." Little did I know how soon I would eat my words.

PicNic pulled up outside a small bar located right on Castro. The high energy music could be heard up the block. I became very excited at the thought of finally dancing off some of the one-too-many beers I had consumed. Rambo had righted himself and therefore looked pretty presentable and PicNic was flawless in his leather pants and jacket - no shirt. So what if our track record hadn't been so good up until now, we were about to have some serious fun. The boys and Stretch hit the dance floor while I went in search of a bathroom. Those beers were really starting to move through me. I searched along the wall, around the bar, even near the D.J. booth but all I could find was a men's room. A very crowded men's room I might add. I looked around at the clientele. Well no wonder there wasn't a women's room, there weren't any women! Maybe it was a slow night for women, after all it was a Friday. Oh well, I had been places before where there wasn't really a women's bathroom and from working at Mikes I certainly wasn't shy if it was an emergency and trust me, this was becoming an emergency. I entered the men's room which was small and basically boasted of one huge urinal. I think it may have had a stall but the line was so long I never actually got sight of it. Never mind, nature called. I was a sport, I figured there were worse things in life than figuring out how to use a urinal, so, preparing for the task at hand I dropped my drawers like the rest of the men and took my place at the font. Just then, I was grabbed by the tiniest little man I had ever seen.

"You cannot possibly piss in this urinal!" he screamed in an amazingly accurate falsetto.

"Well," I said trying to reassure him, "It isn't one of the easiest ways I've pissed before but I think I can manage."

"That's not what I mean. I mean I can't allow you to use this room because you are a woman."

"Trust me, it wasn't on my list of things to try for fun but I failed to see the women's room, maybe you could show it to me." I said politely.

"We don't have a women's room," he snapped back, "but follow me." He led me through the maze of people back to the bar where he muttered something to the very busy bartender. My bladder was bursting by now and so I almost missed seeing the giant doughnut key chain that the bartender passed to this little man. Key in hand, the little man, who was obviously the cocktail waiter, led me through the maze of people, around the back of the dance floor, down a hallway to a little door that opened up into a room that was no bigger than a utility closet. As a matter of fact it was a utility closet!

"This is how it is," the little man sneered. "I am very busy and I don't have time fo this. I'm going to lock you in here and when you're done, you knock and I will let you out. Then, from now on, when you have to go you will come to me and when I'm not busy I'll take care of you."

I was horrified but I complied gratefully as time did not permit for argument. It was a different story when I rejoined PicNic however. Both he and Rambo tend to be the biggest feminists I know and when they heard about what happened they were really outraged. Apparently a bit too outraged because the D.J. overheard their comments and suddenly PicNic was 86'd for putting his jacket in the 'wrong' place. There we were, out in the street yet again. Now group patience was wearing thin.

"Well, I'm sorry that happened to you, Barmaid," Rambo said patronizingly, "but I bet if we were to go into a women's bar the same thing would happen to me."

"What, they'd lock you into a utility room with a doughnut key chain?"

"Well, I bet they wouldn't have a separate men's bathroom."

"How much?" the beer was obviously talking.

"One hundred dollars," the Blow Jobs were talking louder.

"Fine, you're on." Foolish lesbian pride screamed.

We looked in the phone book and found the bar closest to where we were. Francine's it was called and as we made our way down the block to the doorway I began to sweat bullets. I needn't have, as we walked in the bartender smiled broadly at all four of us and welcomed us to Francine's.

"Do you have a men's bathroom?" Rambo openly challenged.

"You bet," said the bartender, "it's right down there next to the women's room."

PicNic ordered a beer and took off his heavy leather coat while I followed Rambo to the bathroom to collect my money. There it was, a real men's bathroom complete with a urinal and everything.

"You see, Rambo," I said rather authoritatively, "the women here have gotten over this separatist bullshit, they have come to realize that we are all Gay and so we should stick together... they are tired of fighting the other half of the populat-" he was just handing me the hundred dollars when we heard the ruckus up front, it sounded like PicNic and he was in trouble!! We ran out into the bar just in time to see a woman, not as big as PicNic but twice as butch, getting ready to lay him out.

"What happened?! What happened?!" I cried out to the woman.

"He took his jacket off and exposed his hairy man-chest to my girlfriend!!" The major butch cried out indignantly.

Jesus, this had not been my day. I am normally a pretty quiet person and being thrown out of bar after bar was just getting too weird. I decided to show everyone that things could be resolved peacefully and quietly without a scene and without getting thrown out. We were going to have a normal vacation if it killed me. I took the two women aside to talk with them quietly and smooth things over.

"Look girls," I started diplomatically, "my friends are not from here and where we come from guys take off their shirts all the time,"

I don't exactly know what happened next, I think I blacked out right after the butch started to say "No, you look Blondie" All I know is that apparently, I caused the biggest scene of all. It must be true however, PicNic is not the kind of man that locks women in the trunk unless it's absolutely necessary. As for my excuse, well, I don't really have one. Like I said from the beginning, it was a vacation from hell... the only thing I can say is, vacation or not, Nobody calls me Blondie!

# ROLES WITH HONEY

## A Modern Fairy Tale

Once upon a time—maybe yesterday and maybe not—there was a lesbian whose name was Little Red Riding Butch.

Little Red Riding Butch lived in a fairly close-knit community where she was known by lots of people. she was an unpretentious woman who practiced herbal motorcycle repair and was frequently seen wandering about in the woods collecting all kinds of helpful holistic medicine.

She was called Little Red Riding Butch because of her always-worn flannel shirt, a bright red shirt with big black checks which was mated with the standard Levi's 501s. LRR Butch always had a stack of keys attached to the loop of her jeans, and was perceived as a boyish looking lesbian, mostly because that is how she desired to be perceived (although, if truth be known, she had a very vague stirring, a thought not yet formed, that revolved around silken fabrics, or something like that).

One day LRR Butch was in the woods stomping about in her logging boots, short hair held in place by a cap which said 'BOY' in big letters, her face freshly scrubbed and void of all unsightly "girly" make-up. As she stomped, she ran smack dab into the ol' Not-so-Big, Fairly Androgynous Wolfie.

"Well Hi there," said Wolfie rather sweetly, which came as a surprise to LRR Butch. She had heard stories about the Not-so-Big, bad Wolfie down at the local bar on many a Saturday night.

"Hello." LRR Butch carefully smiled back, as she knew the Wolfie was quite dangerous from all accounts.

"What are you doing out here in the woods all by yourself?" asked Wolfie rather innocently.

"I'm collecting some herbs for Grandmother Butch so she can make a decent motor oil for my motorcycle," explained LRR Butch rather guardedly.

"Really, how interesting," said Wolfie, not at all interested. "Mind if I walk with you for a while?"

LRR Butch thought about it and then—as if she were on the verge of a great discovery and against all of her inner warnings—exclaimed, "Well, I guess if you really want to..."

They walked in silence for a while, and then had a few friendly exchanges about herbs and flowers. Wolfie seemed to know a great deal about the woods, a fact which struck LRR Butch as odd since she didn't seem dressed as a typical outdoorsy type. As a matter of mention, she didn't seem dressed as any type at all, which really rubbed a nerve in LRR Butch's body.

Slightly aware of a growing attraction she asked Wolfie, "Are you a Butch or a Femme?"

Wolfie laughed, "Oh, I don't get into that sort of thing. I like to explore both the feminine and masculine aspects of myself."

This confused and scared our Little Red Riding Butch, as she found the concept totally unfamiliar with her own perception of the natural order of things. After all, she had always been a "Butch". Dresses were for another sort of woman. A woman who, upon having a flat tire, would stand by the roadside for hours until someone with tire changing abilities could come along and fix it. A woman who could be seen at the make-up counter at Macey's. A woman who shaved parts of her body.

Sure, she had slept with those types of women, but she would never be one. Wasn't it politically incorrect as well as a lot of hassle for not much reward?

"You seem like a nice woman," said LRR Butch, "What do you possibly get out of exploring your 'feminine' aspects?"

"Well," drooled Wolfie in her softest voice, "It's very hard to explain, but there's a time and a place when getting into your feminine self can be very pleasurable. I'm sure that you will find out someday. Anyhow, I have to be going. It's been nice talking with you."

And with that she disappeared into the shadows.

LRR Butch continued her stomping and gathering, her mind still on the brief encounter with Wolfie. "How strange," she kept muttering to herself, until at last she reached Grandmother Butch's house. She threw her cigarette butt into the burn pile, bent and retied one boot lace, and swaggered to the front door.

"Come in," the grandmother's voice called.

Oddly enough, it didn't sound like the grandmothers voice. It was softer than usual, more mysterious.

Butch entered and found the whole house dark except for candles that were placed sparingly around the dimly lit living room. Grandmother Butch was sitting on the sofa dressed in her usual whit shirt and tie. But there was something different about her.

"Are you feeling okay?" asked LRR Butch, another wave of confusion washing over her.

"I've been a little out of sorts these days but it's nothing serious." The grandmother replied in that same milky voice. LRR Butch had an uncontrollable shiver run down her spine.

"I can come back another time if you are not feeling up to company," she voiced almost eagerly, feeling some type of impending danger.

"Oh no," whispered grandmother. "I've been so looking forward to seeing you. Come a little closer so I can get a better view of your motor oil herbs."

Against her better judgement, LRR Butch moved in very close to grandmother.

"My, what pretty eyes you have today, Grandmother Butch...Are you wearing makeup?"

"Why, how silly of you to say so, LRR Butch, you know I don't wear makeup."

"Yes, but your eyes are so big. I don't think I've ever seen them that big."

"Well," crooned the grandmother, "That's probably because I'm so very happy to see you."

Then LRR Butch noticed something else. She bent closer to see if she was right. "My, how nice you smell today grandmother, are you wearing perfume?!"

"Don't be ridiculous Butch. You know the only thing I wear is musk or men's after-shave." And the grandmother laughed very alluringly.

LRR Butch moved a little closer and looked in disbelief at what was not possible. Surely her eyes must be playing tricks on her!! "Grandmother, your legs look so smooth, like there isn't any hair on them...and under that white shirt you're not wearing boxers—you're wearing panties!!!"

With that, the grandmother jumped up and grabbed Little Red Riding Butch, and in one graceful move, handcuffed her wrists together!

It was the Wolfie!!

She slowly undressed Little Red Riding Butch and carried her to the bathroom where a hot, scented bath—complete with candles and champagne—awaited.

There, amidst much teasing and foreplay, the Wolf proceeded to soap and shave the helpless Butch so lovingly and slowly that LRR Butch half forgot that she was a captive. After the bath, Wolfie gently dried Butch and oiled her whole body with something that smelled like heaven.

Cradling her in her arms once again, Wolfie carried Butch to the vanity and with expert talent applied ever-so-subtle touches of makeup, stroking Butch's face with fingers and lips made of fire.

Blindfolding Butch, she slipped something silky and pleasantly torturous around Butch leaving it undone in front as a promise of things to come. Wolfie combed Butch's soft hair and towelled it playfully until it became rakish and wispy as opposed to stern and straight like before. Finally, she carried the now entranced Butch to the bedroom where, with ribbons and feathers, lips, hands, fingers, arms, and legs, she made mad passionate love to her.

She only stopped once—at a very crucial point, I may add—to demand to know Butch's real name. Butch could not hold back and willingly moaned, "Mary. My name is Mary".

Never had Butch heard her real name said so sweetly over and over again as on that day. Later, as she was uncuffed and the blindfold removed, never had she seen herself look so sensual.

LRR Butch still collects herbs for motor oil, still rides a motorcycle and can still change a tire. She has also, however, been seen on occasion in makeup and very soft fabrics—balance, don't you know.

The grandmother was conveniently out of town that day but arrived back, and upon glancing around her cottage knew that there had been a change. Grandmothers tend to be very wise.

As for Wolfie, well, she hangs out in a variety of places as with her, anything is possible.

If you have any doubts however, check the forest. Whatever your forest may be, she is still wandering there.

Trust me...I should know.

# TROUBLE IN TAHITI
## Or The Carringtons Go Abroad

Vacations are the stuff dreams are made of. And a vacation to Tahiti has got to top the list so when I was given the opportunity to vacation in this tropical haven with my beloved 'Madame X' and her family, how could I refuse? Enter the BIG mistake.

Madame X's family is an odd sort. With too much money come too many aires and a general notion that you SHOULD be able to control the universe as a whole. Being gay does not fall under the heading of good social conduct; therefore it is frowned upon but tolerated under protest (we are civilized people, after all) if you so happen to be the 'Carringtons of Tacoma's eldest daughter. I however, being not a true clan-member but rather a "phase" that Madame X would hopefully grow out of, was not offered the same benefits or treatment that the "real " spouses were given. Hence, it came as no big surprise that while Alexis was paying everyone's passage to Tahiti-*including* spouses, that I would be conveniently left off the guest list unless I could come up with the money to go.

This was no problem—a mere two thousand dollars is so easy to come up with these days—especially if you're working as a cocktail waitress. Perhaps I tend to be stupid. Perhaps I have an overblown stubbornness about showing people that "Gay is O.K.", and any relationship regardless of the gender dynamics should be taken seriously and nurtured. Perhaps I was just being a 'dumb blonde' who wasn't going to take this sitting down. Whatever the reason, I was determined to hock everything I owned to be on that plane, to board that ship, to cruise those Islands as a legitimate family member.

It was 4:00 a.m. when we boarded the first plane toward Tahiti. I with my new tanning booth tan, travel brochures in hand, and four suitcases which included everything from a typewriter to a rubber raft (motor inc.), I smiled triumphantly at my "In-laws". The Carrington women in their new summer frocks looked as fresh as May flowers, while Madame X and myself, in faded Levi's and crumpled shirts, were more like the chickweed in the garden. Undaunted by the politely horrified stares of Alexis, I bounced up the boarding ramp ready to order a tall Bloody Mary.

By the time we landed in Tahiti I was a real Bitch. With delays, laylovers and a terrible James Bond movie which was my only source of entertainment, I had been left with a bad taste of forboding in my mouth. The only conversation I had even been a part of with the Carringtons had ended with the Carrington boys saying "Kiss of the Spider Woman" was O.K. until John Hurt had kissed "that other guy right on the mouth." I felt like a black person at a K.K.K. meeting and I wanted to rip off the pillowcases and then run for my life. "A vacation is a vacation," I reasoned. I was determined to have a good time—that's when I got off the plane.

When the first blast of hot, humid air hit me I assumed we must have been disembarking next to the plane's overheated engine. My God, it was eleven o'clock at night and nothing is 90 degrees warm outside in March at 11PM unless it is an unnatural act of Satan. Tahiti, however, is that unnatural act.

As I stood on the platform looking for something familiar, (like a building) my mind became aware that my clothes had somehow turned into handiwrap and were clinging to preserve the freshness! I had heard all about the heat in Tahiti, but someone forgot to mention the humidity. I was soaked! I saw a small building that must have air conditioning. I made a mad dash for it when suddenly a mosquito as big as Cincinnati began to fight me for my luggage. At that point I was ready to give it to him too, as it weighed at least 75 pounds, but just then he saw that Alexis had Perry Ellis designer bags and left me to haul my duffle bag in peace.

The air inside the building was hotter than the air outside and a bunch of half-naked Polynesians were dancing and singing like they never heard of air-cooling systems. I decided to clue them in.

"You know you guys could wear shirts if you'd get some air conditioning in here." I said wisely to the fattest of the men. That's when he lei'd me. Great. I come all the way to a God-Forsaken oven, get lei'd by a fat Polynesian man, and it only costs me 2000 dollars.

We were herded like cattle from one bus to another bus until finally we reached our hotel. At last I'd finally be able to spend a moment alone with Madame X. There was only one problem, someone was already occupying the room. I tried to straighten it out with the front desk but no one there spoke English. Finally through a rather complicated series of hand gestures, a Tahitian woman said something that sounded remarkably like "Stupid American Pigs" and gave us a new room. The view was so romantic. Madame X and I stood on the balcony together overlooking the water. It was like a movie; suddenly she turned to me, stepped close and whispered "There's my family down there in the cabana, let's go have a drink with them."

I bought the "family" a round. I was feeling rich because the man who exchanged the currency at the airport made a gross mistake and turned my 100 American dollars into 11,000 French Polynesian dollars, that's when I found out that a beer costs 650.00 dollars in Tahiti. I was so depressed that I wanted to go back to our room but Madame X decided she wanted to stay with her family. Inside the room I started looking around. Some romantic vacation this was going to be: The Madame off with her family, and me sweating by myself.

I found a bunch of tiny bottles of alcohol (the kind you get on airplanes) in the refrigerator. I decided someone must have left them behind when they checked out, I also decided to drink them all before whoever it was came back for them. I had never heard of a courtesy bar before, it cost me another 4,000 dollars.

The next three days were like the first. The two weeks on the cruise ship was anything but the Love Boat. I mean the scenery was o.k. but the company left something to be desired, mainly because there was *no* company. I became increasingly aware of the fact that with 22 heterosexual Carringtons on board there was very little chance for romance between me and the Carringtons eldest daughter, especially given the fact that Alexis, who had made the cruise ship arrangements, had conveniently ordered a room with twin bunk beds!!! Oh well, it didn't seem to bother Madame X anyway. Her goal on this vacation was to find a way to be really accepted into the group. She began to assume the air of unattached...straight woman??!! No this couldn't be!! I was being paranoid simply because everything was geared for the straight couples...Nobody—and certainly not Madame X—would be fooled into thinking that the grass was greener on the other side of the bed!!! How dare I be such an idiot!!! This was all just "romantic vacation blues"—everything would be fine once we hit our own turf again where we could be supported as a couple...I mean, sure it was hard not being able to hold hands on deck, dance together in the ships disco, put our arms around each other for a romantic picture from the ship's photographer. It looked so much easier to be straight—but NO!!! NO ONE would realistically just switch!!??!!! I couldn't believe how turned-around I'd gotten. I had come on this trip to let everyone know that this relationship was serious. That I couldn't be so easily discouraged and daunted as to stay away from my mate just because the family didn't approve! Heck Dang! Why Madame X had been gay longer than I was, how ever could I possibly think that she would be so easily swayed???!! Silly Barmaid!!!!

A month after we got home Madame X became attracted to a man. Tahiti anyone?

I've still got the travel brochure. It shows a beautiful woman, tanned with long legs sipping a cool, frosty drink on the white beach. Beside her is a man...of course. There are also two other couples on the beach. Two men with their arms around each other watching the waves and two women sitting close together studying a shell.

—So what if I had to glue them in the picture myself?

# WHY BE PROUD OF BEING GAY?

## Gay Pride. Gay Pride.
## What To Say About Gay Pride?

It's not that I don't respect the concept of Gay Pride. I guess I've just always had a bit of trouble understanding it.

I remember at 21 I attended my first Gay Pride March. It wasn't called a parade back then, although it looked like a parade to me.

Seattle's version ran down Broadway and up to Volunteer Park. At the end there was a bunch of music and speakers, but no one could hear them because it was a sunny day and everyone was running into people they knew or were attracted to, or ex-lovers they were trying to avoid.

I thought Gay Pride was about the courage it took to be in such a large group of people while watching a parade disguised as a march that I did not understand. I was naive then. I thought that all of these Gay people must have sincerely believed that a bunch of non-gay people were going to come up to Capitol Hill to see them display their Pride.

I had no idea that year, that some of these marchers would, on Monday morning, go into their workplace and still never mention their lover, their place to socialize, their sexuality.

My second year, I was older. I questioned why. What is Pride anyway?

When we have a march in our own back yard for us who already understand our lifestyle because we are experiencing it, how hard is it to be proud?

39

I decided that year to put Pride to the test. First, I told my parents. "Mom and Dad, I just wanted to let you know that I am still Gay and I am really having a good time now that I know a little bit more about who I am."

That sort of worked. I mean, I wasn't exactly proud of being Gay. That wasn't an issue, but I was proud of being honest with two people that I loved.

I decided to try it at work. I went to my boss and announced, "Mrs. Taylor, you and I have been working very close together and just so there is no big surprise in the future, I think it only fair to let you know that I am a Gay woman..."

It was an interesting discussion, and she really seemed genuine in her questions.

That Sunday night I was called by a secretary and told that there had been some cut-backs and my services were no longer needed.

I wasn't hurt and I wasn't mad. There was a certain amount of relief knowing how someone felt about the real me instead of the one-third of me I felt safe in sharing.

I was proud of myself again. Not for being Gay—that still wasn't the real issue. I was proud for taking a risk, for being willing to open up, and for not being angry at someone else's reaction.

After all, when you give someone all the information, the decision is still entirely theirs.

Finally, I tried treating my lover like a lover in public. My reasons weren't exactly because I was proud to be Gay, but more like I was proud to have that depth of feeling and emotion for someone.

Perhaps behind my back there were frequent jokes and cruel comments about two women being so intimate. In my mind, people would have been no less cruel to a substantially overweight man, a cripple, a spastic, or a person with a deformity.

Our culture is just set up to fear what is different, and to ridicule in order to reduce the fright inside.

That's when it dawned on me; it isn't about being Proud to be Gay, just like it isn't proud to be straight, or white, or thin, Jewish, Mormon, a shoe salesman, a Mom, or a Priest.

That is just one of the many things we are.

I myself am proud of who I am, not just about the gender of the people I sleep with. I am proud of the things I've accomplished, the lessons I've learned, and the people I've touched positively.

I am also proud of the community in which I exist, not because they are Gay, but because they are fine human beings who try to be sensitive and help one another. They are committed to doing good works and working to alleviate the negative stereotypes that were created in the past.

As for our Gay Pride days, perhaps it's just me, but I've always seen them more as Gay support days.

That's when we all get out there and cheer each other on, love each other, hug each other, and just be there for each other. I would like to see a few more of those days *en masse*. I think they are so very healthy for all of us.

Last but not least, the issue of Gay Pride itself.

I remember a time when everyone who was Gay was really fighting to be recognized as a total human being, not just a Gay person. Our arguement at that time was that we were tired of being thought of as Gay first, then a friend or a brother, a co-worker, a hairdresser.

We fought very hard to remind people that we were a hell of a lot more than just Gay.

Maybe, instead of centering our pride around being Gay, Straight, Bi-Sexual, Transexual, Unisexual,( or as Rita Mae once said about herself: "Pansexual"), maybe we should have a Self Pride Day. A day to be happy that you are Gay, but to be proud of your ability to be honest with yourself. To be proud that you made a choice to go with your feelings no matter what the consequences, and that, as hard as it was, you followed through.

I guess all of this can be summed up in one little thought I just recently had...

Loving the same gender is wonderful and at times exhilarating, but loving yourself, your dreams, your choices and the way you deal with others...

Now that is something to be proud of.

# THE BURNING BED

Remember when you first met? The luminous glow that was in his/her eyes as you had your first conversation? It was about art wasn't it? Or poetry? You both lingered over dinner (expensive dinner) and wine (vintage wine) while you spoke of your views of life, love, and...togetherness.

He/She loved broccoli—what a fated coincidence! Long walks were a common passion, and you must have been the only two people in the world who read that quaint little book, oh what was its title? It didn't matter; you were on the same wave-length, obviously.

Love? It must be, but also something more *real*, more cosmic! *Fate* had brought you together and there was no stopping it. You must be as one. We're talking the big ticket, you know—living together!

Oh, how happily the two of you tripped down the garden path toward a life together! It was like something out of that quaint little book only the two of you had read (what *was* the title of that book?!!). Anyway, there you went, into the romantic sunset together, you knew it would work, you loved everything about each other. Well, everything you knew about each other after three weeks, anyway.

But now let's change the scene: Somewhere in time, six months later. Let's look in on the honeymoon cottage. As we come up the garden path we can see none of the yard work has been done in, oh, about five and a half months. Trouble in paradise? Nonsense; there must be a good explanation.

Inside the cottage there are cigarette butts in all the ashtrays. Sweetie-pie had promised to give up smoking! Hmmm. Looking around the cluttered apartment (it didn't seem too small for two people when you first moved in!) we see that someone likes French Provincial furniture *very* much. Somehow we guessed it isn't you.

Suddenly on the sofa we see your beloved. He/She is asleep on his/

her back, mouth open with a little stream of drool oozing out. Isn't that cute?! Well, you used to think it was adorable when you first were together. On the kitchen table are last night's dinner dishes. And look—someone didn't eat the broccoli! He/She hates broccoli? That's not what she/he used to say, now is it?

Finally we see you. You are holding an automatic pistol and madly burning Zane Grey paperbacks. You can't take it anymore you say? He/She wasn't any of the things that you thought he/she was? It was all a farce?

Now we feel very upset for you. We didn't know it was going to turn out this way, or we would have never looked in on you. We like believing in fairy tales and happy endings with no work. Tsk, tsk.

We have just decided to leave when you stop us at the door. You want to tell us something. A secret. You say you are moving out while your beloved remains asleep on the couch. The gun is only in case sweetie wakes up before you are gone.

You smile now and tell us the biggest secret of all! Things do work out, you say. Why just last week you met the *real* person of your dreams! This time you have everything in common. No, really?! The two of you have even read the *same book?!*

We are happy for you. Very happy, really. Won't we come look in on you after you've settled in? A pleasant invitation, but we think not. Why not? Never you mind. But thank you for asking.

Just one more thing. We sure wish you could remember the title of that book.

# SPRIΠG FEVER
## Date And Mate

It has been said that in the spring a young man's fancy turns to love. Well, I wouldn't go that far. As a matter of fact, I believe it is actually more of a base response, you know, a waking from that winter hibernation.

Yes, that's it.

'Long about March the old blood begins to stir and gay people all over the world begin to wake up and sleepily stretch their limbs. The cave, complete with VCR, Microwave Popcorn and a stockpile of taped late night movie classics is abandoned in search of something else, another need...an almost intangible need.

What is it?

Wait! We know. We remember this feeling from many Springs past...a lover!! A mate!!

That's what it is! Of course!!!

Great. Now that we know what our primal instincts are calling for, our civilized minds have to deal with the execution of getting our needs fulfilled.

This does not make us pleased. What ever happened to the more simple times, we ask ourselves. Those times long past when we as man with needs would just emerge from our caves and go grab a mate from some rock, mutter "baby, its you" in guttural cave man sounds, and throw our chosen mate down on the ground for a romp on the wooly mastodon.

Those times are long gone, we reflect sadly. We have shed our bear skins for Bill Blass originals and Anne Klein creations. Now the mating ritual is a complex dance full of intricate steps which involve washing the car, dining at fine restaurants, and trying to carry on interesting conversation.

Ahhh, progress. 'Tis the nature of the beast, that little tempest inside of us is really raging now—insatiable is a good word—and it is fast becoming the word of the day. Reluctantly, we decide to get a move on and begin going through all the phone numbers we have collected in that alpha state that we were in when we socialized that one day in December.

Okay. It isn't all those phone numbers. It's one phone number. It's one phone number so hastily written that we are not even sure of the name scratched on that bar coaster.

We dig out our new-age bear skins and, without thinking, dial the number written on the coaster. After many uncomfortable seconds we hear a voice on the other end of the line.

"Be charming, be witty" we tell ourselves.

"Hey, it's a beautiful day, and you're a beautiful person, how about a beautiful evening with me."

The voice on the other end of the phone sounds confused, even unwilling. You try and explain. "I met you at...(there is a pause while you turn the coaster over praying to god that the name of the bar is on the other side. It says *'Vote for Crystal Lane'*)...that bar where they were passing out 'Vote For Crystal Lane' coasters."

The voice on the other end sounds even more confused. Now you are really confused yourself.

You hope the operator will do an emergency interrupt but you know that only happens in those late night movie classics you have stockpiled. Simultaneously you both realize you are talking to your potential date's mother. Geez, now you really want to hibernate.

"Well, can you just give them the message that so-and-so called. I would appreciate a call back at their earliest convenience."

There it's done. Now you do your hair and sit next to the phone waiting. It wasn't that bad. You can get into this dating thing. It just takes a little effort that's all.

After five hours the phone rings. It's your prospective date and they sound excited. "Do you remember me?" You ask cautiously, a wave of panic hitting your stomach as you realize you forgot to wash the car.

"Of course I remember you. How could I forget...."

You are elated. And then self-assured. How could they forget you. Damn straight how could they forget you. You are a wonderful human being, full of life and amazing qualities. Why you just might be the best thing...

Your thoughts are interrupted by the date-voice...

"You're the one who needed an accountant to do your April taxes. I gave you my number and told you to call me when you had everything in order, did I explain my fee?"

Accountant? We're talking to an ACCOUNTANT? We did our hair for an accountant?

"Right," we say, trying to recover. "Well, I just wanted to let you know that I'm still not ready."

"That's okay," counters the accountant. "Actually, I've been pretty busy myself. It's spring, you know."

Later, as we are going over our list of old classic movie titles that we taped all winter we say, "Fuck it". We decide to go outside and make a huge barbecue.

Maybe, just maybe, the smell will attract some primal neighbor.

Happy spring and buy your briquettes early.

# LOVE AT FIRST NIGHT
## Or Moments With Mongo

Ah, summer! Ah, romance! It's that time of year when everything is in bloom. The boys in their colorful Bermuda shorts, the girls in the boy's colorful Bermuda shorts (except at Women's bars, ladies, where black and white is never out of trend), tank tops, no tops and convertibles with the tops down. Summer barbecues abound, tasteful beach gatherings (be selective here) and lest we forget, the BAR SCENE!!!

It seems that summer is the time for true party pigs to don their flashy summer wardrobes and go on the big game hunt—that's right, the number one safari.....the biggest trophy animal of them all— Chance meeting/TRUE LOVE!!!

Sound familiar? No, not you. Not me either, but for those silly few, those silly, mere 10,000 that this could apply to—Enter "MONGO".

Mongo doesn't have a real name, His/Her pseudonym may be Larry, Joe, Cathy or Mo. Sometimes it's hard to recognize Mongo. Mongo is usually well-dressed, but there seems to be a roving look in his/her eyes. Pay attention to that look. Proceed with caution!! MONGO is armed and dangerous—to your bank account!! O.K., Barmaid, get more specific!! It usually starts like this.

You're at a lovely cocktail lounge (well, maybe just a gay bar); You can be alone or with friends, but the point is you're looking. Someone catches your eye. They have made a *point* of catching your eye. You smile, they smile...you look away (coy thing!), they come closer. In a voice that would mash avocados, they croon, "Would you care for a drink?" This is a crucial point. Is this the first drink of a beautiful relationship, or... The Kiss of Death?! You go for the drink (I know you!).

Mongo introduces him/herself. Enter line #1.

"I rarely come to these kind of places; I just hate bars. You see, I'm a homebody." At this point it would behoove you to ask whose home—but of course you don't. instead, you flash those brown, blue, green, hazel or odd color eyes at Mongo and pull out your wallet.

"Let me buy you a drink," you offer. Mongo has already flagged down the bartender and ordered a Tia Maria Amaretto with a Baily's float. It comes to $10.50. Mongo flashes you a smile and you forget all about the $10.50 and the next ten $10.50's. The evening progresses, you have Mongo right in the palm of your hand. Mongo seems really taken with little ol' you!!! Imagine that!!! Since things are going so well, you ask Mongo if she/he would like to leave this "Bar scene" and go somewhere less crowded. Mongo speaks. Enter line #2.

"Well, what I'd really like is to have you over to my house for a nightcap... but my roommate is, well... kind of... well, you understand." Of course you understand! You're an understanding kind of person. I've got an idea!! Why don't you invite Mongo over to your place!! Dang! You're too quick for the old Barmaid! You've already done just that!! And Mongo, believe it or not, accepted!! He/she just had to go behind the bar to get something...it's his/her suitcases. You leave the bar together, each carrying two suitcases, get into YOUR car and head home. Mongo stays the night of course. The next morning, he/she needs to borrow your car keys... he/she forgot they had to work this morning. You didn't really want to lend your car, but it is Mongo after all.

Later, some friends ask you to go to the beach. Since Mongo isn't due home from work for a while, and you have already finished making your famous Chicken A La Idiot for tonight's romantic dinner, you accept. As you are driving up to the beach, you recognize one of your old friend's cars—no wait!!! That's YOUR car!! And there's Mongo on the beach working on that famous Mongo-tan!!

"What's going on?" you demand.

"Wanna beer?" he/she asks taking off the walkman (a very familiar walkman).

"I thought you were supposed to be working?"

"Did I say working? I meant looking for work, but it got way too hot for pounding the pavement."

It is at this point that a few lucky souls have had sense enough to grab the car keys, check Mongo for stolen credit cards, and run like hell.  There are quite a few others who haven't had nearly enough fun yet and choose to marry a Mongo.

If  you haven't yet had a treasured "Mongo" experience, take my advice and continue to avoid one.  If on the other hand you've ended up marrying one, do not fret.  It has been my experience that these marriages, while expensive, don't last long.  You see, Mongos seem to have a  very short life span.

Hmmm.

# TOFU SURPRISE

Relationships. The rod of hope, the bread of truth, the staff of life-sometimes a staph infection. At least so says your Barmaid. How many of us have invested in a priceless human being only to find out that we were doing our shopping under the blue light at you-know-where?

Relationships. It takes at least two of us—that's 50% more dangerous than reading a book. And for what? Less time in the bathroom? Shouting matches at 3 A.M.? Cover stealing, TV hogging and a reason to over-eat? It just doesn't make sense to me. Especially when in the end it's the same old thirty days notice, either them or us, the Hatfields and the McCoys. Pretty depressing when you put it on paper, isn't it?

It isn't you? Hah! Statistically, one out of every two people can identify from personal experience with what I've just said. If it's not you, then take a peek at your better half. I'm afraid there's no getting around it, although I did try once. I went to see an old Lesbian mountain woman (who lived in Tacoma, WA) to ask her how to keep a lover. One that would grow and learn, one that could be trusted, one that wouldn't suspect what an ass I am.

Her tent was pitched haphazardly against a big stucco coffeepot structure known as Bob's Java Jive. Outside the doorway a large neon sign read, "TRUTHS FOUND, WISHES GRANTED, TAXES DONE. STEP INSIDE." Well, since I hadn't brought my taxes, darn it, I guess I would have to settle for a wish. I parted the flap of the tent and was enveloped by a powerful blast of Goldenrod smoke. Now, I didn't know at the time it was Goldenrod smoke, but it came up later in the course of conversation. Her name was Tofu Surprise, and she was as old as the bean fields of Mexico.

I smiled nervously at her and started to tell her what I had come for. She shook her old grizzled head and said, "I know what you are looking for; you want someone. Someone who hasn't been around the block as often as you have." (Not that I've been around the block, mind you.) "Someone who doesn't know how to play nasty games."

Yes, that was it!! The old woman had hit the nail on the head! Now if only she came about five-foot-ten, blonde, 120 pounds with a tan and a sports car, I'd be set!!

"This is not easy," she continued. "Many people have come here looking for the same person..."

"Other Lesbians have asked you for the same person?" I questioned.

"And gay men and drag Queens and Mormons," she replied. "Joe D'Maggio even stopped here once for the same reason, but I guess he misunderstood my advice. I get about 359,000 people a year all asking the same question. It gets very tedious."

"Well, what about you?" I asked. "Do you have a lover? The kind that everyone is looking for?"

"Nope," stated Tofu flatly. "I don't want one either."

"But it's the American Dream!" I shouted. "Don't you have *anyone*.? Someone?!"

"Well, I have a cleaning lady that comes twice a week. It gets pretty messy in here with all of you crying and using up all my Kleenex on the he/she done me wrong song. The cleaning lady is a real sweetie. Sometimes she does more than the cleaning, if you get my drift."

Great. So there I was talking about love and relationships with a Lesbian Guru who didn't even believe in them and would frequently womanize her cleaning lady!! "My point," I said, keeping my voice as level as possible, "is can you help me or not?"

"Of course, " she chuckled, "if it's what you really want."

"It's what I really want," I snarled.

"Okay then; here's what you do. You find yourself a real young one, just coming out, and when you've picked the one you want, I'll do the rest. Deal?"

"Deal," I agreed. I left her tent smelling of Goldenrod and went to seek my mate.

Two weeks later I found her. She just happened to be looking for the same book as I was; she needed hers for a college class (perfect). It was her first year. She was here on a theatre scholarship, had graduated from high school at the top of her class and didn't know anyone from here yet. This was her! I could feel it. She was gentle, unpretentious, fun-loving, humorous, and drove a sports car. This was the fresh, trusting lover that Tofu had promised.

Three weeks went by, and then it happened. Katie (that was her name) fell deeply in love with me. I don't mean "in-love" the way two mature adults fall in love; I mean that first, magical In-Love that you look for the rest of your life, the kind you wish for...Wish for? Hey! That was it! It was all Tofu's doing. Hmmm. I guess that was all right; it was what I had wanted after all. Now Katie wanted to live with me. Before I could give an answer on something that important, I decided to go see Tofu one more time to make sure the spell (or whatever it was) would last.

When I got to her tent, I noticed something was different. It took me a few seconds , and then I realized what it was: no Goldenrod smoke. Very strange. I stepped all the way in, and before I knew what hit me I was staring at the most intimate parts of my beloved Guru. She was dead. Her skirt was pulled up over her chest and there was a smile on her face that ran from cheek to cheek. Also, the tent was spotless. (How considerate of the cleaning woman!)

I had been so stunned by the preliminary sight that I had almost forgotten why I had come. Now it didn't matter. I couldn't get an answer anyway. I guess I would just have to figure it out for myself. It was a simple question really: Do I trust Katie to be a part of my life knowing now that she is wonderful but perhaps not bewitched? She could be in control of her own decisions. She could be making her own destiny and choosing me to be a part of it. Do I risk it again with someone, knowing that this might be a relationship that, although under no spells or magical chants, might have just as equal a chance of surviving? Do I take that risk, fight that fight, trust that trust? What would Tofu Surprise, the wise Guru, tell me to do? Better yet, if she had it to do all over again, what would she do?

That's when I realized people have to follow their hearts. Advice, even when well meant, can be ill spent. Yes, following my heart was the only way to go, and suddenly it all became very clear. I knew what I must do.

I bought that tent next to Bob's Java Jive, learned to smoke Goldenrod and read a lot. See, my heart said to me, "If it doesn't come with a guarantee, we don't want it." Maybe that's how Tofu got started, I don't know. One thing I do know, however: she sure has good taste in cleaning ladies.

# "MY FUNNY VALENTINE"
## Or "Cry Me A River, Bitch!"

I'd been out until four in the morning dancing, drinking and having an absolutely wonderful time trying to forget that the next day was St. Valentine's Day.

It's now one o' clock the next afternoon and I've just gotten out of bed—alone. My eyes try to focus as I am lighting my first cigarette, the sole companion to my automatic coffee maker, both conveniently located next to the bed. Suddenly in bright red letters with hearts and arrows it's that day again, boldly embossed right there on my daily planner. 'Today is the day to buy flowers for that special someone,' the cheery Hallmark inscription reads.

"I'm single," I scream at the mocking inscription, "and I love it!!!!" I start thinking about my recently ended two year involvement with the Dragonlady.

"What a ridiculous thing to be upset about!" I murmur to myself, remembering how I know all of the counselors at the crisis center by name. "So what, it ended...so what?! I'm free, blonde and know how to tie a tie! I'm champagne without the headache!...Roses without the thorns!...Calvin without the Klien!...Calvin without the Klien?!"

Anyway I am feeling great about me, great about being single, great about the day and great about the Dragonlady.

"You know" I say to myself, "It is Valentine's Day. That poor Dragonlady has probably just been sitting around pining away since we split up. She probably realizes what a mistake she made,...how much she misses me...what I meant to her. I should give that ol' gal a call, let bygones be bygones. Nothing she says will affect me anymore. I have nothing but warmness in my heart for her." I pick up the phone...

STOP! Does this sound familiar? Can anyone relate? It's called "Hey, I feel pretty good about myself; I think I'll give the 'ex' a call," syndrome.

Let me personally illustrate the guidelines that this disorder usually follows:

The phone is ringing. Suave doggy that I am, I have already lit my third cigarette, completely forgetting that my second one is still in the ashtray unfinished. It will probably cause a four alarm fire later in the day.

The Dragonlady answers.

"Dragonlady?"

I of course do not call her Dragonlady in real life, but for public purposes I choose to protect the innocent...me of course.

"Yes." She sounds like she has been up all night.

"What have you been doing all night—last night I mean." ('Good recovery, Barmaid,' I think to myself)

"Oh I was out with friends," she answers.

"What friends?" I ask casually. There is an undercurrent in my voice that sounds remarkably like Bette Davis in *What Ever Happened to Baby Jane?*

"Oh, you know, The Unicorn Woman and Seven Sisters College." (these are also fake names.)

"Well how fun." I say genuinely. I am genuinely relieved because both of these women are straight.

"Yeah, I had a GREAT time!" (What does that mean??!!) 'GREAT time' usually suggests women of the same sexual orientation....you know, Lesbians!!!! A cold fear starts to creep up my spine...

"Where did you go?" I asked with fearful anticipation.

"Oh, you know, Women's bars."

"But there's Lesbians there!!"

"I know that, Barmaid, that's why I went."

"Really?" I say, "How nice." (there is enough strychnine in my voice to kill the whole cast of a Cecil B. DeMille movie.)

"Well thanks Barmaid," She says casually.

"So," I say (because there is no more room for niceties), "Did you meet anyone?"

"What's that supposed to mean?!" (okay, its open war.)

"You know what it means, *did you meet anyone?!*"

"So what if I did?" she says.

"Well I want to know," I counter.

"We're not girlfriends anymore," she snaps.

"I know that, duh," (I haven't used the word "duh" since third grade, but it seems appropriate for this occasion.)

"Well, if you knew that, then why are you asking me about my PRIVATE life?"

"C'mon!" I whine (I know I can get to her if I whine), "Just tell me."

"No." (did she really say that?)

"Please!!!" (It's a good thing she can't see me because I am jumping up and down in the living room like a wounded chicken.)

"Barmaid. Are you jumping up and down in the living room like a wounded chicken?" (God I hate people who know me so well.)

"No, I don't do that anymore," I answer haughtily, "I am a mature woman now."

"Well, I'm glad to hear that," she says sweetly, "I always thought you could be." I decide to ignore this last barb and pursue my direct goal. "Who is she?" I ask.

"I'm not telling," she counters.

"Dragonlady, just tell me, I'm not going to get upset so just tell me!!!" (I am screaming into the phone).

"No, I am not going to tell you...But you can guess...."

'Fuck-off,' I think to myself. I don't have to take this. It's not that I give a hoot either way anyhow. I was just trying to make conversation. Who cares who she's interested in sleeping with....I mean, so what...?

"Do I get a hint?" I ask trying to stop my hands from shaking.

"Okay...Ummm...Peter Pan."

"Peter Pan? What does that mean? You're going to sleep with Sandy Duncan?! But Dragon, she's nearly blind and besides I heard–"

"Barmaid. It's not Sandy Duncan."

Reality hits. No of course its not Sandy Duncan because it is a beautiful French Goddess. A beautiful French Goddess who just flew in from St. Tropez. She is cultured, she is sensual. She wears layers of soft Irish Linen and talks ever-so-softly. I can picture it now...The two of them sitting at a candlelit table, sipping cool glasses of fine white wine. She leans forward, her long legs showing and whispers, "Dragonlady, I think you are majestic." (The one word I have never called Dragonlady, drat it all!) "I want to be with you...Soon..." Her eyes are mesmerizing...she leans closer....Dragon's lips are quivering....

"Barmaid?"

"Huh?"

"Are you still guessing?" The vision of this mysterious Goddess still on my mind, I answer sadly, "I don't think I know her."

"Oh, of course you do," she say's cruelly.

"I do?!" Immediately I start processing information faster than an I.B.M. "How do I know her? When did I meet her? Does she have any distinguishing marks or scars? Is she a friend? Is she really young? Did she ever go out with anyone I know?" I point an imaginary finger-gun to my head, "Did I introduce you?" Suddenly it all came together. The mysterious St. Tropez Goddess disappears as reality punches me like a heavyweight boxer."

"No!" I say.

"Who?" she asks.

"No!!" I say...

"WHO?!" she asks.

"It can't be!!!" I say.

"Why not?!?" she snaps.

"Is it?" I question.

"WHO!!?" she screams.

"It's Flasher, isn't it?" I state.

"Yep," she answers flatly. The whole thing is horribly anti-climatic.

"I don't believe it," I say softly, "The women is a pervert."

"Oh, how would you know? " she snaps.

I think back to the time when Flasher started seeing my dear friend Red while Red and I were house sitting. I didn't even know Flash, but her naked body was endlessly lounging around the house. Besides putting a dead fish in my bed, breaking into my bedroom and rubbing ice cubes all over my sound asleep body, wanting to freeze everyone's tampons and showing me her most private parts while discussing how things may have been higher or lower-longer or shorter than average...well, I guess I had no reason to call her a pervert. Did I mention that she kept insisting that my three month old puppy knew how to do things with a woman it took me nineteen years to try?!!!! I and my friends saw Flasher naked more than we ever did with clothes on. Other than that, I suspect she was a perfectly normal girl.

I tried warning Dragonlady, she became angry. I tried reasoning with her–she became angrier. I tried being complacent and feeling like shit, this seemed to make her feel better.

"Dragon, the woman is a pervert!!" (I couldn't help myself).

"Shut up." she said. I sank lower into my old couch with no springs. We talked about the weather, about dogs, families and having lunch in time. I wished I lived in Bora Bora. I even searched through my mind for how much of this was jealousy and how much was genuine concern. It came out 50/50. I decided I would be less concerned and more jealous if it had been Sandy Duncan after all. With all the couth I could muster, I carefully ended the conversation.

Sitting alone in my house I thought of the Dragonlady being attacked in the middle of the night with ice cubes. This woman helped me get my first credit card. She taught me how to get my first drivers license and how to eat Mexican food without picking out the onions. She taught me how important it was to have a matching bathroom set...

So what if she needed 14 hours of sleep nightly? So what if her favorite art form was made-for-TV Harold Robbins novels and her favorite color was vibrant purple, it was still no reason for her to have to wake up with a dead fish in her bed. I got up leaving my sixteenth cigarette to cause a four alarm fire and went into the bathroom (yes, the one with the matching towels) and put on sackcloth and ashes. So much for feeling good.

Since then I have talked to Dragonlady once or twice. She and Flasher have been going out and having "a wonderful time." Well, there's no stopping progress I guess. I have come to one conclusion from all of this that I'd like to share with those of you may be in similar circumstances.

There are three things I recommend doing if you feel the urge to call a new ex-lover:

1. Don't.
2. Have your therapist standing by.
3. Move to Bora Bora.

# YOUNG AT HEART

A great number of gay people seem to have this issue with age. Youth vs. Maturity. The young in age within the gay community are either chased down like deer in hunting season, or shunned completely. Either way, it's not like we *listen* to them. Children should be seen and not heard.

Anyone older seems to encounter the same type of attitude from the young.

"Troll" is frequently a word used for people over 35 seen out in the bars, and God forbid someone that age comes over and tries to fraternize with the 21-25 crowd. The lust for young firm bodies is evident on his/her face as he/she talks about the opera, skiing, or property taxes.

I remember this attitude very well from my own gay "childhood." Not only did I appear on the scene at a bare 20/21, but I insisted on becoming involved with a person fairly well established in the community who, of course, happened to be ten years my senior.

It was a match made in heaven (so I thought), and the Dragonlady and I had everything in common.

There were a few minor differences. Things like she had a drivers license and I didn't. She required more sleep and hated early morning cartoons. I was still in school, but it was college—and a lot of people go to college. The point was that we were in love, so nothing so petty as our little difference in age was going to come between us!

No Way!

Actually, I admired the fact that she was older. I had never slept with anyone who could have actually driven themselves to Woodstock or who remembered what a "love-in" was.

It was fascinating.

She learned things too, I believe. New Wave became more than just a term for a different kind of greeting, and she found that the stereo speakers wouldn't distort if you turned the volume knob all the way to half up.

She bought hair gel. I bought wrinkle cream. She went dancing. I went to the museum. We made love for hours and then finished off with some wild sex. I thought she was class incarnate. She thought I was complete high spirit.

Everything was perfect and so we decided to share our friends.

The first time I was introduced to a group of the Dragonlady's friends, they asked to see my I.D. I realize that I have always looked young for my age, and at 21, I probably passed for 16. But I remember how much it rubbed me the wrong way that someone had asked for my I.D.—in a private home.

Dragonlady was my lover, not my babysitter. I was an adult capable of making mature decisions.

The rest of that evening I sat sulking with my glass of kool-aid, popping my gum and wondering why the Dragonlady didn't defend my honor. Boy, I knew my friends wouldn't behave that way!!! My friends weren't *age-ist!*

The Dragonlady apologized later, but the wound was already made. Her friends thought I was a baby.

"Chicken" they called me. "Cradle Robber" they said to the Dragonlady.

I decided I didn't like them. They were old and boring and not any fun at all. They didn't know who the B-52's were, and they still wore polyester.

The Dragonlady wasn't like that. She was secretly too young for her birth certificate. That was it!

I decided she would have a much better time with my friends. They were more her type anyway. They would love her and see in her exactly what I did. Young people are just more open to new experiences, I reasoned.

The first time she met my friends was at a dance bar. I thought she looked great and was going to make a fabulous impression.

"How old is she anyway!?!" One of my friends asked boldly. Another friend looked right at Dragonlady and said, "Do you remember the war?" (they meant World War II).

After hours of stupid conversation about whether or not Joan Jett was really a lesbian, Dragon politely asked if we could go home. I realized my friends had not made anymore of an impression with her than her's had with me. We decided that the way to handle things was to just keep our friends separate.

And so it began.

She would meet her friends at quiet bars for cocktails, I would meet up with my pals for beers and dancing. Dragon would have great telephone conversations about writers; I would have great telephone talks about whether or not Joan Jett was really a lesbian.

The more time went on, the further and further we pulled apart. I didn't want to stay home at night and watch David Letterman, and Dragon didn't want to go out bar-hopping and drinking 'til dawn.

What was happening to us, I wondered.

She liked T.V. I liked discos. She liked walks at the arboretum, I liked rollerskating around Greenlake.

I started to think we did not have anything in common. She would be much happier with someone her own age and me with mine. At least that's what our friends kept telling us.

Subconsciously I began to create a break-up. Consciously it worked.

Two and a half years blown to smithereens all because of an age difference.

That was about eight years ago. Now I am just about the age that the Dragonlady was when she first met me. We are dear friends and equals. Through the myriad of friendships and relationships I have had since that time, I have come to realize that no one is ever completely grown. The trick is trying to grow together and giving permission for individual expression.

I am now very close to a young woman who is about the same age I was back then. Funny, but she is nothing like I was at 21. It would be easy to dismiss her opinions, her creativity, and her zest for life just to being young, but I understand now that a person of any age has value and many things to teach.

Yes, I have learned torn Levis and "Big Hair" are "Narley" and nowadays the volume control on your stereo can go 3/4 the way without distortion. But she has learned there is such a thing as required sleep, and the Joan Jett debate is at least ten years old.

It's not just about differences. We also have a lot in common.

Take the year 1968, for instance. 1968 was a very special year for me. It was the year I took my first plane ride, learned all the words to "Satisfaction" and memorized my times tables.

1968 was a special year for "the kid" too. It was the year she was born.

# THE LUNATIC FRINGE

Lovers. Everybody wants a lover, a Valentine, a sweetheart just like the one that married dear old dad. And why shouldn't we? We are geared from our earliest existence to believe that we should come in pairs, (which, as far as that goes isn't a bad idea). We see it on television, in commercials—why they even sell toilet paper as a couple type thing. We are led to believe that we must be a twosome in order to be normal and happy; after all, as the media has explained it, we brush to get "Close Up" to someone else, we wash our hair so that Joe on the second floor will notice the shine and ask us out, we even buy shoes from Volume Shoe Source so that we can have enough money to go bowling with Ted. Get Real!! Have you seen Ted? He's a fat guy in a dirty white undershirt, drinking beer in front of the T.V You would never dream of Ted as your knight in shining armour unless... and wait because this is the clincher... unless the alternative is—BEING ALONE—

There, I've said it. The second most treacherous "A" word in the English language. ALONE. Salt without pepper, bacon without eggs, Cleo without Patra. Alone.

It seems that this time of year is the worst time for feeling the pressure of being uncoupled as well. It becomes a frantic search for Mr./Ms. Right and why? That's what I don't understand. What's the big deal?

Last week I decided to get to the root of this frenetic coupling phenomenon, and so I asked a group of single, searching bar patrons why they wanted couplism so much.

"Someone to sleep with, someone to hold", "Someone to go to movies with." "A person to come home to." "Someone to buy presents for..." These are the answers I received that day and it helped me identify the whole situation. These people didn't quite understand, if they want all of that and just that (minus the movies)—get a dog. No really!!

Now you probably think that I'm being very flip but take a look at the future. Six months down the road, for instance, that dog is not going to fight you for the remote control to the T.V, or think your a weird jerk for giving concerts in your bedroom wearing only your underwear. Hey, the dog loves it when you drop food on the rug, leave piles of clothing on the bathroom floor, turn the heat up to high and watch T.V all day. The dog doesn't care if you gain 10lbs, forget to buy fruit juice or don't get home till 3:00 a.m.

People tend to have this misconception that lovers are cuddly, sweet, thoughtful, and a joy to be around 24 hours a day. Ha! That's not lovers; that's new dates. There's a major difference, like about 6 months!!

Being a couple doesn't just involve having someone to sleep with and share special little moments with. Oh, no!!! True, we're led to believe that that's what goes on, but let's take a look behind the scenes—

A day in the life of a normal couple usually begins with the morning coffee. The morning coffee has changed somewhat from the old days where your new love used to bound down the hallway to get that automatic drip dripping. Remember how sweet it was when they made that little detour to the bathroom and brushed their teeth, combed their hair and bounded back to the bedroom, steaming coffee in hand, to shower you with kisses. Times have changed just a bit.

Now your loved one rolls over, with squinted red eyes and hisses with serious morning breath, "Hey babe, you know where the coffee filters are, don't ya." Eventually the dead rise, and a shower is in order. Remember those freshly laundered towels? Yeah, well, they went out with the special soap about two months ago. Now it's the crumpled green towel and the dwindled bar of Ivory. There's no shampoo in the bottle this morning either. Honey-poo used it up yesterday and forgot to buy new. Hmmm. Do you venture a kiss? Months ago it would have been a definite *yes* but now you are not so confident. Wasn't it only yesterday that your true love had squirmed impatiently and croaked "Not now honey, I'm trying to read the sports page." And then we have breakfast. You have long since given up the hoax that you both like all the same foods—you're content to let your mate drink the Java, down a leftover egg roll and rush out the door toward the nine-to-five. Remember how hard it used to be to leave them for work in the morning? The smile on your face as you head out the door tells us that you've gotten over that little business probably about the same time as the towels—but hey, you do an eight hour stretch at the office and poof, you're ready to do that couple thing again. Now you meet your honey for an evening which consists of bantering back and forth about what to do tonight, until nearly exhausted, you order a pizza again and fall asleep in front of the T. V.

Oh, yes, I know when we tend to want a mate we are thinking of the glamorous aspect, the constant *togetherness*, not the *constant* togetherness.

My mom always said, "Be careful what you wish for, you just might get it."

So at these special times, when it seems only right that you should link up with life's greater moving force, look at the pizza box on the bedroom floor, look at the pile of clothes in the bathroom and that big empty corner in the living room that is just right for a canine companion.

# S/M THANKSGIVING
## Or "Pass The Whipping, Please"

November of '83 wasn't unusually cold. It wasn't unusually warm either. In fact, the only unusual thing weather-wise was the unusually strong wind on Thanksgiving Day.

Nothing to be concerned about unless you were planning on traveling or cooking on a stove. I myself had no intention of doing either. Today I was a guest. I had done my little festivities the night before by hosting an all-out community event known as "The Annual Thanksgiving Gay-la celebration." As a result of this fabulous party I received both a black eye and tore some ligaments in my leg, thus preventing me from helping with today's feast in any way. It was my duty to sit most painfully on the couch icing my ankle, while watching the Macy's parade on the T.V. The woman I was seeing was most gracious as were her two charming roommates, Lorna and Lisa. I was really enjoying their company and wished they didn't have to leave, but they were expected elsewhere. Now, looking back, I'm sure they must be glad they left.

Some things you don't expect on national holidays. Some things you don't expect even if they walk up, slap you in the face, pinch your butt and announce their plans to ruin your whole day. Then again, some people are oblivious to fate. I am one of those people, I know that now, but hindsight is cheap, they say.

When 'Mooncycle-crystal-woman' (you know how I get carried away with my code names) invited me over for a "family style" Thanksgiving, I should have paid more attention. I should have watched her eyes, listened for any unsteadiness in her voice, suspended a bare light bulb above her head and made her take a lie detector test while interrogating her mercilessly about this so-called "family". But

'Cycle' was a nice woman. It didn't enter my head that she could do anything less than wonderful.

Yes, I knew she had a lot of different friends. I knew that some of her friends were into S/M, but I had recently done an article about S/M women and found the people I had interviewed to be both intelligent and concerned citizens. I did knit my brows together when Cycle told me the 'Grim Reaper' was making the turkey, but it was pot luck, after all, and just because a woman looks anorexic doesn't mean she can't cook.

At 4:00 p.m Thanksgiving day I became concerned. Where was the Grim Reaper? Where was the turkey? Cycle said the Grim Reaper was probably sleeping because she had been tenderizing the turkey the night before. Now I consider myself a fairly open minded woman, but this did not prevent visions of this poor little turkey being chained, slapped and whipped until the meat was at the desired tenderness. "Get over it, Barmaid," I said to myself and laughed at my stereotypes. Two hours later I was waiting expectantly for the turkey in bondage to appear no matter how stereotyped it may be. You see, by this time there was so much black leather in and out of the room, I thought we were having an eclipse.

"Okay, dress is dress." I told myself. "Lots of people wear black leather...James Dean wore black leather...Cows wear black leather...Well, sort of...." I tried desperately to not be one of those women who pigeon-holed what they had not experienced.

"Stop this," I said to myself. "Okay, so it's not over the river and through the woods, to Grandmother's house we go...It's not over the leather and through the whips yet either!" What was I expecting to happen anyway? Naked dancing?...Free whippings for all???—God, Barmaid, that's only in the movies! Perhaps I was just missing the "old family Thanksgivings." We never had the B-52's blasting on our stereo during the holiday festivities. We never consumed a case of Lowenbrau per person, and the closest we ever came to the wafting odor of marijuana was the one year my mother surprised us all by acquiring about two pounds of sandalwood incense (on sale from K-Mart) which she promptly lit all at once. Needless to say, we had Thanksgiving at Denny's that year as we waited for our home to air out.

I decided to halt my misgivings and just settle down to a good time. After all, I couldn't walk, so it wasn't like I was gong anywhere quickly.

Besides I trusted 'Cycle.' She had assured me she wasn't into S/M, and since I was "seeing" this woman that's all that mattered. Suddenly, with much cheering and whoopla, in walked the Grim Reaper carrying a tin-foiled turkey...and a pillowcase.

"What is in the pillowcase?" I asked nervously. No one answered me—they were all too busy cheering. Nasty toys—I bet myself. I hate pain, I realized but once again, just as my imagination was running full-force downhill, I discovered my fears were unfounded. The Grim Reaper promptly dumped the contents of the pillowcase onto the coffee table and as I pushed my way through the crowd of wild, excited women, I saw...a pound of baby powder?! I limped away, disappointed. "I bet we're all going to have to powder our mashed potatoes or something weird," I thought cynically, but I was wrong.

QUESTION: What could a bunch of grown women do with a pound of baby powder?

ANSWER: They could inhale it up their nose with little straws!!

"Strange tradition," I mused as I went to see if the turkey really was tied down after all. Dinner was ready, Hooray!!! I was starving!

"Dinner is ready!" I screamed. Nobody moved. The guests were all sitting around the coffee table, engrossed in this baby powder. 'Burning Bush-head' was saying, "Good stuff, good stuff" over and over again. Everybody seemed really into the baby powder. Personally, I thought it might be painful.

I decided to eat. I was one of four people who made the same decision. As I sat at the head of the table, a huge, almost untouched turkey as my companion, I looked out into the living room. There were almost all the guests in one big happy circle and here I was with the food. I felt sick knowing how much I must look like Henry the Eighth. Why, I wondered, didn't anyone else consider dinner the main event. It was like everyone had lost their appetite at the same time...It was as if a strange power had consumed the whole living room at once...it was as if..as if..my God!—It finally dawned on me! I couldn't believe how naive I was. That wasn't baby powder on the coffee table, I was looking at the world's largest stash of COCAINE! My mother would just die if she saw me now.

"I knew she was hanging out with facist lesbian drug addicts!" she would say. I tried to think of the orange sherbet so she couldn't intercept my thoughts. I knew my face was falling off from shock, so I decided to go into the living room and look open and cool.

"So what's new?" I said in my best Neil Diamond voice. Everyone looked up and stared. I sat down on the couch and fell into the part with no springs. I was praying the cat would come by and cover me up. No such luck.

I thought I would have to do something like have an asthma attack or faint or talk about Idaho or something, but just at that moment my good friend and co-worker 'Leggs' and 'Spike' both greeted me with hugs and kisses, taking special care not to get me wrapped in their chain. They were chained together for the holiday season.

"Look who we brought with us!" Leggs chirped. I gaped around them and saw a women I recognized as 'Flame', an intelligent pre-med student and erotic dancer on First Avenue.

"Flame is going to do a dance for Thanksgiving!" Leggs announced.

"Great." I said, still being ultra-Neil-ish. I noticed 'Snake-woman,' Flame's old girlfriend, wasn't pleased. She was staring hard at Flame. I turned to see what the problem was and noticed that explicitly naked, women's parts were gyrating just inches from my gaping mouth. My teeth snapped shut so loudly that it sounded like the lockdown at Monroe State Prison.

"She's great, isn't she?" Spike sighed. I don't remember what I said, but I think it sounded like "orange sherbet". The other women were cheering wildly, and it was so warm in the room that the pumpkin pie had melted 20 minutes ago. Just when I thought nothing else could possibly happen, someone else screamed.

"You did so well, Flame, you deserve a whipping!"

"Yes, a whipping!" everyone chimed in...everyone but me that is, I was still chanting "orange sherbet".

"I'd love a whipping," Flame crooned, "But did anyone bring a whip?" All of the leather women were looking at each other with that 'whose got the ball?' look, when suddenly Cycle-woman, my current "date" piped up—"I've got one!"

The last thing I saw before I fainted (it was too many pain pills, of course) was the sly smiles of the S/M women who stared at me, knowingly.....

# WITCHES, WARLOCKS, RAMTHA & THEE

The other day I came across a magazine. It wasn't just any magazine; no, this was a New Age mail-order magazine for anything from crystals with magical powers to a book with "practical advice on how to initiate yourself as a witch and start your own coven." The magazine came bulk rate, in a plain, brown wrapper from—you guessed it!—Salem, Mass!

Now maybe I'm a spiritual prude; maybe I'm even a bit too old fashioned and conservative. But the fact remains that I don't like the idea of chakras, bio-rhythms, healing crystals, and magic wands all coming by mail from some warehouse in Massachusetts.

I am not so caught up in modern vogue as to pooh-pooh the power of any occult science. And as far as witches go, I have learned through experience to have a healthy respect for anyone who is practicing what is commonly called "the craft." I remember back before Ramtha spoke. Somewhere after Stonewall but before "Lipstick Lesbians" got in full swing there were lesbian witch-women. They didn't write books, they didn't give public forums 400 dollars a weekend, they still don't live in fancy houses built from their crystal jewelry mail-order business. No, these women were fairly private about their religious beliefs. The community knew they were out there; it was understood that if you had a problem you could always go to so-and-so who would offer some comfort, herbal tea, and a tarot card reading to help get things clear. Very few times did I ever see money exchange hands with these women, and if so it was for such a small amount that it probably barely covered the herbal tea and incense. There were house blessings, purgings, cleansings and many rituals between friends. An altar was a private thing then, not something that you'd see featured on *Good Morning America*, and crystals were a private source of energy—something you searched for, went out of the way for. Maybe a witch woman made it for you; maybe you made it yourself. Whatever the situation, it wasn't fashion jewelry! The real witch women are still out there, but nowadays so is everyone else.

I suppose all of this wouldn't be so bothersome to me if I hadn't run into "Sibyl" the other day. Her name didn't use to be Sibyl; it used to be Buffy or Bunny or Tippy or something. I first met her a couple of years ago at a bar. She was a lesbian from Bremerton, and she wanted to get into the Seattle scene. Her outfit (if you could call it that) consisted of every piece of hardware that Ernst might dream of carrying, all quaintly wrapped in the equivalent of two hides of leather. There were more straps, buckles, and chains than you could find in the US Doberman Training School.

I foolishly asked her where she got her outfit.

"Oh, I made it up myself," she explained. "I heard the women in Seattle really go for the leather thing, so I wanted to make sure I got noticed."

I tried explaining to her that leather in the women's community was more than just a fashion, but to no avail, I noticed that quite a few women must have had the same idea because now even housewives from Mercer Island are cleaning house in knee-high Nazi boots and bomber jackets purchased at Nordys.

Sibyl didn't stop there—every time she heard of a trend that was supposed to be "ultra lesbian," she plunged into it full boar. I remember the day she pulled up on her new Harley, the summer she grew tofu and wheat grass, joining the women's gym, and the last time I saw her she had become a witch. Her house was painted entirely black inside. There were fifteen altars throughout the house with everything from magic wands to shrunken heads.

"Sibyl, are you sure you know what your doing?" I asked.

"Sure," she answered, "I got directions with everything I ordered."

"Ordered?" I felt very strange knowing this air-head even possessed half the stuff. Now she was saying she ordered it, leaving me with the sinking feeling that any crazed maniac could get this stuff through the mail.

"Yeah, see anyone can order this stuff through the mail. Here's a book that tells you how to make people do whatever you want them to. That's what I'm practicing now. After that, I'm going to try and summon up a spirit. Maybe I'll steal Ramtha from you know, what's her name."

I looked around the house. Sibyl was an air-head, but she was not alone. How many other people had altars in their basements or attics and were conjuring up spirits in their spare time? Maybe this stuff was all harmless, maybe not. But should it be readily available? "Secrets of the underworld" is not exactly what I hope my hot-tempered neighbor is reading in his spare time. Perhaps I had been spoiled. I had only been exposed to people who, if they practiced this form of religion, respected all sides of it. Leaving Sibyl, I realized those days were probably gone forever.

What's in the future? I suspect that soon Mercer Island housewives will be chanting over dinner, stirring the soup with their crystal wands. Nordstroms should come out with their own line of magic perfume called, oh, how about "Nordstrodomous"? Black will continue to be an all season color, and you should be able to call up a spirit of your choice with nothing more that a computer software package made exactly for this 'New Age'.

As for me, I have a healthy respect for what I learned at my great grandmother's knee. She has always believed in "another plane." Even before deregulation, Grandmother taught me not to trifle carelessly with such things. Still, it's a tempting thought to summon up someone like Ramtha—for my next story.

# PARIS IN THE THE SPRING

Her name was Genevieve. Genevieve Truelove. I shall never forget the name.

It was a beautiful spring day. The kind of day that made you think of long walks on the beach, sipping cool drinks just before sunset, and lots of suntan lotion. I was working inside that day—daydreaming, pretending I was another person in another place (a detective, I think, somewhere along the lines of Humphrey Bogart), when in walked my fantasy. She was wearing a low cut slinky evening gown, red with a deep brimmed panama hat—women's cut—which hung mysteriously over one eye. A long, slender Tiparillo floated gracefully from her gloved hand, connected by a slim jade cigarette holder.

"Help me," she whispered. "My child, she is missing."

"Have no fear," I assured her. "I can solve your problem, Miss—?"

"Genevieve, Genevieve Truelove".

And indeed she was. Like in all good movies, I heard violins and saxophones, and like in all good movies, I knew I would not accept her money, not in the end. We would marry instead and blissfully drift into the sunset.

"We must have meetings," I informed her, "To discuss details, of course."

"Of course," she said. I saw a faint smile of things to come.

The days flew by with whirlwind speed. I met with Genevieve daily. Sometimes we walked along the water, other times we sat in small cafes where Sam played it again and again. Although we kept our talk to business, all the signs were there, and I knew that she had it bad. The coy glimpses from beneath her hat, the way her dress casually slipped slightly off one shoulder from time to time and that smile, always that promising smile.

It was a Friday, two weeks later that I found her child and reunited the two of them. The case was over. Early Saturday morning I received a phone call. It was Genevieve.

"Barmaid," she whispered. "I know you don't owe me anything, but I must see you. I have to tell you something that I have wanted to say to you since the moment I first saw you." I knew what she wanted—this had always been my favorite part of the movie. She would confess her love for me, and we would float effortlessly off into the sunset.

"Yeah," I said chewing on the butt of my cigarette, "I can meet with you, what time? Where?"

"How about this evening for dinner? At Blochs?"

Okay," I said very nonchalantly, "But it'll have to be around seven." I didn't want to seem too eager.

"I'll be looking forward to it," she whispered.

That evening I put on my best overcoat, a nice London Fog, and walked the seven blocks to Blochs. I had made sure to give myself a bit of time so that I could be waiting casually. I was 45 minutes early, and Blochs was closed down. I sat on the curbstone admiring the evening, the sun hanging low in the evening sky, a balmy breeze blowing lightly across my strong jaw.

Suddenly a loud explosion rocked the sky. I reached for my revolver, but unfortunately it was only a misguided crow who had landed simultaneously on two separate electrical wires. Ooops. I was reminded of my superstitious grandmother who firmly believed that witnessing the demise of a bird was a *bad* omen.

Just then Genevieve drove up. "Hop in," she smiled. She looked fabulous. She was wearing the same red evening dress all satiny and clingy, and her flowing golden locks whipped rakishly against the wind from the open top of her Porche. She chose a quiet, out-of-the-way lounge called the Canterbury.

"Barmaid, I have something to tell you, something I've been longing to say." She ran her finger around the edge of her wine glass seductively and leaned forward, breathing heavily. Outside I was as cool as a cucumber, but inside my veins were pulsing with excitement.

"What is it that you've been waiting to tell me?" I motioned gently, urging her on. At that moment she placed her hand on mine, looked deeply into my eyes and said, "I don't eat pork; my boyfriend is Jewish."

80

Bam! Reality struck me in the face full force! I looked at Genevieve. She wasn't wearing a slinky red dress: she had on sweat pants and a tee shirt. Her hair was cut very short and was dyed orange. And her car was a battered Volvo. I stared out the window at the Canterbury into the pouring rain. Yes, there was a dead crow out there, but I was no detective. I worked at a vet's office, and her "child" was a mean-tempered calico with a chronic case of diarrhea.

I stared at Genevieve the straight woman, who was still taking about her Jewish boyfriend as she drank her Miller Lite. She didn't have a clue. I politely waited until I found a way in and then excused myself—something about needing to get home and write an article.

On the way home, I pondered what I had learned. First, things are not always what they seem. Second, daydreaming can be harmful to the ego. And finally, women named Genevieve may have a natural immunity to spring.

P.S. Does anyone named Linda or Suzi need a good detective?

# ADVENTURES IN OLD MACEDONIA

The other day, someone very close to me asked for some advice. They were in quite the pickle. This person apparently had a long term relationship that was going "alright" up until one evening a tall, mysterious, intriguing, intelligent (need I go on) stranger introduced herself and proceeded to take up mental residence from that very day into my friend's thoughts. The Stranger (who rather pragmatically mentioned a similar attraction for my friend), was just getting over a long term relationship with a person who she wasn't getting over but, hey, isn't that just life? And last but not least, my friend's lover, who is a firefighter, knew almost zilch about the whole thing because she was off fighting fires. Of course, she may pick up this book in some small logging town, but since she doesn't read, I'm not worried. Okay, so now you know the character background and does not the problem become obvious??? It's the age-old conflict that all of us have gone through whether single or attached, sexually active or celibate, old or young...I'm talking about desire, I'm talking about consuming attraction, I'm talking about the most common internal conflict in the world- "to dance or not to dance?" Metaphorically speaking, of course.

I thought about my friend's dilemma. She had met a woman who was more like the woman she imagined being with than the woman she was really with or at this time (because of fires), without actually. Are you following me so far? Good. Now, the other woman, the Stranger, was no longer the woman she wanted to be with or would have wanted to be with if she had been more like some other woman that she could be if she really tried and so she was spending time with my friend perhaps trying to know if she was more like that woman that she imagined her other woman could be, but there was some type of attraction between them and a very strong one on my friend's part. Being moralistic and good, my friend was doing her obligatory "guilt and confusion" penance which, of course, were tempered with thoughts of sheets, skin, and Sweden. I knew where she was at, mostly because I have been there before myself. I was not about to tell her that, however, or give her advice based on how I handled the situation. Instead, I went down to my archives and found, believe it or not, an old legend from Macedonia about a kingdom of Swedish Lesbians who flourished during the time of the Crusades and about a horrible tragedy between four women that started with simple attraction.

Once upon a time, during the Crusades right after squeezable mustard bottles had been invented, there was a kingdom of Swedish Lesbians. Now, whether it was politically correct or not, they were a kingdom. And they had Kings and Queens and Princes and Princesses and knights, etcetera, that were all women. Well, at that time, there was a young King (because she had made herself King) who had become discontented with her old life and castle, so with much ado, abandoned it and her Queen and went in search of a better amusement (although she did stop by for an overnight visit every so often). That was in west Macedonia. In another part of the country, however, there was a notable Prince (Prince because she was a Prince of a gal) who was known throughout Macedonia, as were the King and Queen. The Prince had taken herself a Crusader for a partner and mate against most of her advisors strong wishes. They knew that the Prince was an artist with a quick and hungry mind and that the Crusader, while a peach of a gal, was just not into learning new things or exploring or questioning. She liked the Crusades and sex. At the time, the lonely Prince thought that this would indeed be more than enough and so moved the Crusader into her area of the kingdom and into her heart.

At this point in the story, it is important to note that the village psychic had a terrible prediction about this particular union between the Prince and the Crusader telling the Prince to wait because the perfect match was just around the corner. "Do you know, the only type of woman that could possibly catch my eye at this point would have to be such an impossible combination, she couldn't really exist!" shouted the Prince. "She would have to be well-read, long-legged and stable. She would need an analytical mind as well as a sense of humor. She should be social when called for, enjoy drinking coffee, abstain from elixirs, strange roots and seeds. She would need to be open to understanding the mechanics behind writing and maybe even be an ex-teacher, and last, but not least, a Queen." The Prince felt pretty safe in saying these things because there couldn't possibly be anyone like that out in her realm for surely she would have heard of her by now.

Shortly thereafter, she met the Queen. It was bound to happen because, like everywhere else in life, the phrase "Be careful what you wish for..." holds true, even in Swedish Lesbian Macedonia.

Even though the Prince tried to avoid the Queen and the Queen really didn't pursue the Prince, fate will be fate and soon enough, they had engaged in sparks of conversation intriguing enough that they both agreed to visit further.

So while the Crusader was off crusading and the King was off trying to get a group of people to call her the King, the locked away Queen and the Prince (of a gal) spent time getting to know each other and liking it. They both knew there was an attraction running and being the good and noble people they were, they objectively spoke of it. Because the Prince was involved with her Crusader, she knew that she must not act on any attraction. She had made a vow to her Crusader to wait and so wait she must. It did not occur to the Prince that people change. Perhaps she had outgrown the Crusader or perhaps she just wanted some other input or values in her life...Perhaps not. Anyway, she never thought about it because she had made a vow and for honor's sake, she would keep that vow.

The Queen's story was not similar, but no less moving. She was loyal to her King who had left her, the lands and the castle to find herself and date other women. "Maybe someday when I find myself..." the King would say, dangling the phrase in front of the good and naive Queen. It seemed to work. Her bed was always freshly laundered and empty, as was her heart. She would wait to see if the King would come home, but in the mean time, she would enjoy the platonic company of that lovely, reserved Prince (of a gal).

They spent lots of time together and everything was going along fine until one day, while having a very intellectual conversation about Yugoslavia and eating rolled Wildebeest, the Queen, in trying to figure out the mechanics of twist-top squeezable mustard bottle, had burst the top and was wearing yellow mustard upon her wrists. The Prince casually glanced over intending to view the mess and that is when the thought hit. "Mmmmm. ...I'd really love to bite her skin." The thought completely shocked the Prince who, up until this time, had been irrevocably pure in thought and deed. Well, as pure as a Prince can be. She pondered it. Why? She had seen temptation in many forms and had been unaffected. Why now? Why the unawares, locked in love Queen? She thought maybe it was a fluke, but sure enough, when she looked over at the Queen it happened again! The Prince didn't want to bite her skin hard, no, no...quite the opposite, and other little half-thoughts came to mind as well. All day and all night she had this feeling and because of this she dared not look at the Queen. The next day back in her own realm, she searched her mind for understanding. There was none. It was definitely just the *Queen's* skin that made her feel this way and it wasn't so much just the skin as the fact that it covered the Queen that seemed important. There was a kindredness there that was unexplainable and, of course, biting her skin was just a metaphor. Day and night, she pondered this thing and then knowing herself and knowing morality and righteous behavior, she decided as always to continue to be a Prince (of a gal) and never bring this up. The Crusader had told her many times that she would perish from a broken heart if the Prince ever went from her and so the years passed with the Crusader crusading, the King searching for herself, the Queen waiting for the runaway King and the Prince spending time in the company of the Locked in Love Queen, never telling her that she truly desired to read her a bedtime story, hold her close and maybe even bite her skin—just a little. It was the perfect example of upstanding behavior. Everyone in the kingdom praised the Queen and the Prince for the mature way that they had handled the attraction; and years later, they both died, three days apart. The Prince had long ago sealed her desire both in order to remain faithful to the Crusader and because of fear of the unknown. She died never telling the Queen of her thoughts which probably would have been very good for the waiting Queen.

The Queen, of course, passed away wondering about love and life and still questioning whether or not the King had made it home yet. The Crusader did not die when the Prince was gone, quite the contrary. She had long ago felt a separation between them, but did not know what to say. "She was such a passionate Prince, once," was all the Crusader said. Little did the Crusader know that the Prince had long ago felt the need to bury her passion because of an unruly attraction and, as it is with passion, you either leave it flourish or you tie it down, but you can't have both.

The King was still out dating and finally met up with the Crusader who was still crusading, and together, they began an attraction that, of course, they pursued to the fullest.

Eventually, the Swedish Lesbians died out altogether in Macedonia and are hardly ever spoken of, except in rare circles of upstanding, morally righteous women that meet for coffee while waiting for reluctant lovers.

After my friend read this story, she asked me what the point was. I told her the same thing I will tell all of you: "That, my dear, is up to you."

# MY CAMPING GETAWAY!

Recently I read and was duly inspired by E.F. Strayhorn's article 'Olympic Getaway!' For those of you who haven't read it, it is a moving picturesque description of his perfect weekend vacation in the semi-wilderness of Lake Quinault. His description of the Rain Forest resort sounds so serene and cozy and the outlying area with its "giant awe-inspiring pine and fir trees, towering some 200-300 feet high,....thinly shredded Chartreuse colored cheesecloth delicately hung from every extremity." Well, it just moved me.

I got to thinking. My thoughts revolved around communication and sharing. What a great gift to be able to share that experience with hundreds of readers who might be in the decision making process about *their* vacation.

I thought of my own "Weekend Vacation" taken the very same Friday the 13th weekend as Mr. Strayhorn's. Suddenly I knew that I too had something to inspire those of you who haven't, even those of you that have...and so, Dear Companions, "My Camping Getaway".

The sun slowly rose up and above the majestic buildings that marked downtown Seattle. It was 8 AM Saturday morning, and a nervous excitement filled my already active body and cascaded into the surrounding room. All around me camping supplies waited in abundance for the upcoming trip to the Wenatchee river camp grounds, a do-it-yourself kind of camping spot, nestled sweetly on the banks of the Wenatchee river just outside of Leavenworth.

On this morning, there was great peace inside of me. It was the first time in six months that my lover and I would be having a weekend alone together, just the two of us. So what if only earlier this week she had begun an affair with another woman (to whom I refer as "Oh Her")? So what if last night she had stayed with Oh Her when she should have been home with me making plans about hiking, cooking and such? So what if I had found out she was leaving for California with the other woman on Tuesday, a trip we had planned many times.

I decided to let all those issues slide and was determined just to revel in the glory of nature and my lover (shall I call her Madame X?) for three wonderful days.

What could possibly go wrong? It was a beautiful day, I had all of the camping equipment except for a tent and sleeping bags (those were Madame X's responsibility), and it was only 8:30 AM (She said she'd be here between 8 and 9).

8:53, I saw Madame X's car pull up outside my window (she really made it!) I waved a rather cavalier greeting and began hauling the gear to the front door. My excitement grew. Wow! Three wonderful days to fish, tan, hike and be one with nature, not to mention a beautiful two-and-one-half hour drive in which I'd have plenty of time to ask her what the hell she thought she was doing having—no,no,no! None of those questions. We are going away to have a *good* time I reminded myself.

Smiling and cheerful, I opened the front door. Madame X was standing there "Did you bring the bug spray?" she asked flatly. She looked like something the cat had drug in.

"You look tired Sweetie," I said, (did she notice the unevenness in my voice?)

"Yeah, it was a late night."

'Oh shut-up.' I thought to myself—oops. Peace! Relaxation!

We loaded everything in the car (a Honda Accord) and began our journey to the inevitable paradise that awaited. The drive itself was beautiful with the morning sun glinting off of the tree tops. The mountains loomed above us "Majestic and awe inspiring" as Mr. Strayhorn says, and I wondered about rattlesnakes—both here and in the city. The drive was so peaceful, too peaceful, and I knew it wasn't because of the awe-inspiring mountains, rapture is one thing—Black Death is another story. I decided not to push it.

I played the alphabet game...I made a mental list of things to do when I got home...I counted license plates...

Finally we were at our destination! And so was everyone else who decided to get away for the weekend, except E.F. Strayhorn and friend.

"Damn, it sure is crowded."

"Yes," I said meekly. We drove through the camping areas.

"This road sucks. I'm tired of using my car as a truck."

"Yes," I said again. It seemed to be a safe word.

"I hate camping, you should have called ahead. "Now we'll never find a spot."

"Listen baby," I heard my inner voice say, "*You* picked out the place and *you* were the one who said we didn't need to call ahead. Off my back!" my higher self forced a smile onto my face.

"Sorry dear." (you hair pie!)

We drove down a winding road, over a bridge, across someone's campsite, and suddenly I saw it.

"There's one sweetie!" I shouted

"Fine. How am I supposed to get in there!?" This woman was in a BAD mood. Quickly I thought of fishing and hiking.

"See the road?" I asked innocently.

"That's not a road, it's a cow trail," she snapped.

"Well, then let's pretend we're one big cow," I quipped. (I mean she was obviously having one.)

Bitching and moaning, we wound our way the whole ten feet it took us to get into our campsite. It was a sweet little campsite with an old campfire nestled quaintly among the poison oak. Simply charming. I decided to unpack.

"Before you do anything we should put up the tent and then drive into town for some food. I'm starving. I haven't eaten anything since last night."

"Okay," I said cheerfully. I hadn't eaten in a week, no thanks to Madame X, but hey, the past is the past. Besides I was full of love and forgiveness now that I knew that she had indeed gotten a tent. It was a question I had been afraid to ask.

We unfurled the tent and I waited expectantly for directions on how to put it up. This was no ordinary what-I've-camped-in-all-my-life tent. No! No! This was one of those new-fangled jobbies with little reed sticks that hook together. The kind that bears eat.

"How do you put it up?" I questioned.

"I don't know," she replied.

"Well, where are the directions?"

"I don't know," she said again.

"Well whose tent is it anyway?!" I asked.

91

"You don't want to know." She stared at me...hard.

I tried not to think about the fact that this was Oh Her's tent.

"Fine."

"Well, I didn't have any time."

"Well, of course." I said much too sarcastically. The moments passed. "I'll figure it out," and like a trooper, up went the tent. I relaxed my jaws.

"Shall we go for something to eat?" I asked politely.

"It's too damn hot," she noted as she got into the car.

We found a simple little restaurant in the heart of Leavenworth. Madame X had a hearty homemade avacado/bacon burger with all the trimmings and two deserts. I had a hearty glass of soda water with bitters. Of course the subject of Oh Her came up. Things have a way of doing that.

After a three hour lunch and a quiet conversation, we walked back to Madame X's microwave (the car) and drove to the Leavenworth Safeway. The car was delightfully scented with dead sheepskin seat covers baked by the sun. A most interesting smell. Where was the fishing? Where was the hiking? Where were the rattlesnakes—never mind about the rattlesnakes.

We purchased—or rather I purchased our groceries for the day and as I paid for them, I realized I would need to hit a bank machine for tomorrow and Monday's supplies. I told this to Madame X.

"Tomorrow and Monday?!! I thought this was a *weekend* camping trip.?"

"Listen," I said, " We agreed on Saturday, Sunday and Monday." I was very firm. You see, I have never learned to abandon a sinking ship.

Madame X sulked. We drove back to our campsite in silence. Once there, we unpacked our groceries and decided to go down to the river to read. For two hours we sat by the river. I read. Madame X opted for sulking and staring at me. What a pleasant day!!

Still sulking, Madame X accompanied me back to the campsite.

"I'm taking a nap." she announced. Poof. She was gone.

I sat outside the tent. I gathered firewood. I built a fire. I read the want ads. It was getting dark. It was getting cold. I peered inside the tent. Madame X groaned. I sat close to the fire, and time marched on. Finally it was just too cold. I carefully climbed into the tent; my blankets were on the tent floor as padding in lieu of air mattresses. Oh Her's sleeping bag was to be our top cover. It filled me with great joy, ha ha. I looked for some warmer clothes. Madame X was sleeping on them, apparently Oh Her forgot to supply pillows. I tried to get a cover, any cover. Madame X had them all. A mosquito the size of Leavenworth was looking inside the tent. I shivered.

"Bite one of us and you'll die of poisoning." I whispered. The fire was going out. It will be better tomorrow, I thought. The night passed...slowly.

Sometime in the early dawn, a big white canine wandered through our camp. I took it as a sign for better things to come. Madame X awoke.

"Want some breakfast?" I was so tender.

"Ugh." Yes, Madame X was awake.

"I'll build a fire."

"Ugh."

I scooted outside. The river was beautiful in the morning sun. Leaping and twisting it looked so refreshing I wanted to sit in it—or better yet, throw Madame X in it. I started building the fire. I put two pots of water on to heat once the fire was going. Madame X has to brush her teeth with warm water. I decided to wash my hair. I presumed that after breakfast we'd go hiking and then maybe do some fishing.

I didn't notice that Madame X had crawled belligerently out of the tent. She was staring at the fire. Thinking of Oh Her, no doubt.

"What are you thinking about?"

"Nothing."

Yep. It was Oh Her.

She glared at me. Was that anger in her eyes? "Why are you using all the water on your hair?"

"All the water? We're six feet from the river, for God's sake!!"

"So," she said and went back into staring off into space.

I looked at the hard cliffs glinting early morning sunlight, shooting it down the canyon... up at the blue sky, serene with not a cloud in sight. I looked across the river at the lush, green forest and down at my feet where the dirt was hard-packed and dusty. Then, I looked at Madame X. I doused the fire, I started putting things into the car.

"What are you doing?" she asked.

I stared at her hard for a minute and then I spoke.

"I am not a bimbo. You obviously do not want to be here and I am not the type of person who would want to force you to stay. Let's go home."

Needless to say, the drive home was every bit as splendid as the drive up and just as quiet.

Usually I have a great time camping, and this did not spoil my lust for the great outdoors. However, I have learned one hard and fast rule—If you have a lover who has just taken on a new girlfriend, and you're planning to go away together—for a good time, you had better take the girlfriend along.

As a footnote I'd like to share a sign that I saw soon after getting back to the glorious city, it read:

If you love something, let it go.

If it comes back to you, it's yours forever...

If it doesn't... **HUNT IT DOWN AND KILL IT!!!**

Our city has such a sense of humor.

# SOME STRANGE GUESTS APPEARED TO SOMEONE WHO USED TO LOVE CHRISTMAS

Once upon a Christmas time, I had this friend. Coincidentally, she was a barmaid. A very sarcastic, disillusioned barmaid who just so happened to hate Christmas.

Now, she hadn't always hated Christmas. When she was a child, she really loved Christmas, but after becoming a Lesbian and having several holiday traumas involving lovers around the Christmas season, Christmas just left a bad taste in her mouth.

She seemed to get over it after not dating for two years, but last year she had a fabulous Christmas party for all her gay men friends and as luck would have it, somebody brought her a future X-lover—a rather messy relationship as well, complete with long-distance phone bills, moving and etc.

The "relationship" ended officially right before the holiday season, and so this Christmas she was particularly venomous about the whole concept of "the time of love and togetherness."

One day while she was designing her own line of Christmas cards for X-lovers, (a picture of herself, riding shotgun in Santa's sleigh) and baking Ex-lax fruitcake for the girls, a strange and weird thing happened. There was a knock at her door, an almost hypnotic rapping that the barmaid could not ignore, and so she went to answer it.

There before her stood the most familiar woman—a woman she

could swear she knew although she could also swear she'd never met her before.

"Can I help you?" the barmaid asked dutifully, as she was used to asking this of course, being a barmaid.

"No," the familiar woman said, "But I believe I can help you, I am the ghost of X-lovers past and I'm here to improve your attitude."

"Right," the barmaid said sarcastically. "No wonder you look so familiar. Come on in, but I've got to tell you right now that *nothing* is going to improve my attitude until my X's bite into this fruitcake and that's just how it is."

"Barmaid," the ghost said indulgently, "Christmas is not the time for revenge and I think it is time that we help you explore your feelings about X-lovers and Christmas before you grow old and bitter so that you never love Christmas again."

"You said 'We'. Does that mean it's going to be just like the real Scrooge story and I will be visited by three of you that all show me stuff that will make me cry and change my ways?"

"Well, yes, there will be three of us guiding you, and we intend to show you things about your life and lovers that you may have forgotten, but it is only to help you, and to warn you."

"Okay, Toots, I've got thirty minutes before those fruitcakes come out of the oven, give it your best shot," challenged the barmaid, and with that they were transported to years back when the barmaid was a young lesbian.

"Hey, I know where this is," The barmaid exclaimed. "This is my and the Dragonlady's house!"

"That is correct, and this is Christmas Eve of the year you broke up. You were already on the rocks, remember?"

"How could I forget," she snorted, "Watch what I get for Christmas. I thought it was going to be a moped, what an idiot, hey, here it comes!"

They watched in silence as the Dragonlady wheeled out...

"A laundry hamper! God what a great gift! After that year I made sure to give my lovers laundry hampers to show how much I cared!" the barmaid said caustically.

"Now barmaid, you know what a little pig you were back then, and don't you still use that laundry hamper to this day?"

"Well, yes but..."

"Sometimes there is more to life than just romance."

"I guess. Could we get on with it?"

"Sure, if you remember this place." With that they were transported to a small but cozy living room with a cheery fire and lovely Christmas tree.

"Hey, there's me and Madam X opening our presents. Well at least she was opening hers. Mine weren't wrapped."

"That is correct," the ghost said, "But do you remember why? Hadn't a friend of hers just died?"

"Well yes, sort of. It was a woman she had an affair with."

"Still, you know now how devastating it is when someone you are close to dies. Maybe now you would think about how nice it was for her to make the effort of finding you anything at all and wouldn't have pitched such a fit because it wasn't wrapped."

"I guess so, I'm a little older now."

"Very little. Come on, I'd like to show you one more thing. This is last year's Christmas night. You were working at the bar, but you had just met a woman days before, and it seemed magical. Here is your first kiss together. Look at how surprised and happy you both look. You had finally found something you had been waiting for. Look at the intensity between you two."

"That intensity probably comes from the fact that we know ten months from now we will want to kill each other."

"Don't be sarcastic, barmaid, you know it takes two to tango. Lets look in a little later. Ooops. Not there. You already know that you two were sexually compatible. Hey, right here. Here's one of the times you were about four hours late. See her sitting in the window wondering what has become of you, missing you?"

"Yes I see that. I didn't mean to do that all the time, I just lost track–."

"I'd say you lost track. Well here's the night you didn't go to her graduation from Nursing School."

"I had to work!!"

"It was important to her barmaid. You are a creative girl. I'm sure you could have found a way out of work. And what about here? This is the scene after you two are having trouble and you started spending time with that woman from Canada. Sure you talked about it, and it was clear that you two were slipping away, but maybe you should have—"

"Hold it! Hold it just a second! How come you ghosts always show this stuff? You know, what *I've* done wrong!! How come you're not showing the time the nurse started having a fling with one of my friends, or the time that she ordered me out of the house because I asked her to slow down the drinking?! How come you didn't show all the times that she told me she hated my job or my friends or my shoes or my house or my dogs—or the time she bitched because I took the wrong turn to the fair? How come you don't show the total communication breakdown that lead to my seeing the woman from Canada, or the fact that at times she seemed relieved about it?!!!! Huh? How come you ghosts never show that? How come you don't show the fact that it's hard living in two separate worlds, mine and hers because she only wanted to know me in her world and not in my own?!!! It was damn hard not being able to share my circumstances with somebody that I thought loved me! Damn hard. And I really tried!! How come you don't show that?!!

"Simply because you do remember all that. We're only here to show you the things you are not aware of or may have forgotten, like the meaning of that first kiss. Anyway, my time is up. Now you will go with this ghost. The ghost of X-lovers present."

With that the first ghost was gone. A ghost who kind of resembled the nurse, replaced her.

"Hi, I'm the ghost of, well, you know who I am and so I'll just tell you that (A) I'm not as maudlin as the first spirit, and (B) I'm only going to show you one thing." And with that a scene opened up to them.

"Hey, that's the nurse!!! And that must be her new lover!! Geez, I don't want to see this!!"

"Watch it anyway. I forgot to tell you (C) I'm a lot more butch than the first spirit. Now look. It's been bugging the shit out of you making up pictures of what the two of them are like together. You're not having any fun and you're putting extra stress on people who care about you now (namely one very cute, very devoted Canadian) all because you think this new love is so much better than you. You don't have to buy it and you don't have to feel bad. Take a look. Format has changed, but the movie is still the same—get it?"

"Huhuh, they look like their having fun."

"Of course they're having fun! Remember how much fun you guys had the first couple of weeks you knew each other? Everybody has fun in the beginning. Lighten up! The real world hasn't set in yet.

Now, if they're having fun, doesn't it seem right you should have some fun too? I see a girl who thinks so. Besides, you wouldn't want the nurse to have a horrible Christmas, or would you? Never mind, don't answer that. Now I gotta get out of here so I'm going to leave you with the last ghost, and she's going to teach you a thing or two about this obsessive revenge stuff." And with that she was gone.

The third ghost was exactly like that, a ghost. No form or shape and definitely no warm greeting.

"The future." She somberly said, and pointed.

The Barmaid looked. There in front of her was a huge farmhouse, just like the farmhouse the nurse had always wanted, only better. The nurse was outside in the wonderful rose garden, but she was weeping profusely and saying, "Barmaid, oh, Barmaid" over and over again in between choked sobs.

"Great," said the Barmaid. "Just like Scrooge, I see, you show me the future with the nurse in her big beautiful farmhouse, that she's always wanted in her lovely rose garden, and of course she's crying because I'm dead. I probably died a bitter, lonely woman with no friends except for the nurse who remembers me from long ago. This is supposed to make me change my ways and make me feel loving and giving towards Christmas right?"

"Wrong. Three strikes, you're out. First, that is not the nurse's rose bush. Second, that is not the nurse's house. They both belong to you. Third, you're not dead. You are inside having a hell of a Christmas party."

"Well, why is the nurse on my property, and what the heck is she crying about?"

"Hey, life's rough, you invited her to the party. After we visited you a couple of years ago, you pulled out of the hole, got your shit together, and did everything you said you were going to do, including those best-sellers. The nurse unfortunately wasn't on our list of people to visit, and so we couldn't show her what she'll be missing down the road. Came as a complete shock, and boy could she just kick herself. I always say that success is the best revenge, don't you? Anyway, you're doing quite well, and have gotten over the bah humbug bit and so you're having a big party. Pretty anti-climatic for what you were expecting I bet. That's all I have however, so good luck and work on those novels instead of whatever it was you were baking. I took the liberty of having a piece of that bread after I pulled it out of the oven, and boy was it awful. Now I'd love to stay and chat, but I've got to run—seriously. Good luck." And with that she was gone.

That's what really happened to my friend not so very long ago, and I must say it's changed her whole outlook on X-lovers and Christmas.

"Never let them see you sweat."

I'd write more about the whole thing, but I'm kind of pressed for time. I've got a novel deadline, and boy, do I intend to keep it!!

# THE RETURN OF THE GREEN THUMB

"Lesbian Womyn." The earth mothers. The nature seekers. The all-knowing healers and nurturers. It is commonly known that lesbians possess some secret power, a direct link to the sun and moon which makes them capable of miraculous communication with all living and growing things. Lesbians are the herbalists, the naturopaths and definitely damn great gardeners! I mean, according to all literature I can find, we have to be—it's part of the general lesbian make up. Gardening and Lesbianism is even mentioned in some report I once read, maybe it was the *Hite Report*, although I can't be sure, but it said something to the effect of "...A sure way of discovering whether or not a young woman has Lesbian tendencies is her abnormal interest in other women and her ability to grow all manner of herbs, fruits, vegetables and interesting flowers and foliage." The same report has been updated however and continues to read "...unless you're the Barmaid."

Yes, it's true. I have a brown thumb. I am so bad at nurturing anything that even resembles plant life that I have managed to kill artificial flower arrangements. I don't mean to do plants any harm, but I just don't think I understand their needs. It's not like I haven't tried, either, I have probably spent three million dollars on house plants alone, oh, and my outdoor gardening technique is truly something to behold! Not even weeds want to live in my yard. Late at night I've seen the dandelions trying to scale the fence. It looks like a scene from old footage in Berlin. No, the only plant life in my yard is rocks. Lots of rocks and dirt. In the winter I have mud for a change and sometimes an occasional slide or sludge pond to add visual texture.

I didn't want it to be this way. I'd like a yard with little feminine flowers and trailing this and that. A weeping or wisping treelet would be nice as well, but I don't think it's in the cards.

I became desperate last summer and talked my ex-lover, Madame X into planting some flowers on my property and then tricking them by sneaking over to my house while they were sleeping and coming out on the front porch early in the morning so they would think she was the one who lived there. This worked for a while, but then one day the thriving little carnations out by the front porch saw me answer the door for the pizza man, and the next morning every green thing in the yards both front and back was drooping. Within two weeks it was curtains for the whole landscaping concept.

This plant thing hurts my heart greatly because I feel like I can never be a true Lesbian. Sometimes I even find myself drilling me, asking questions like "Are you sure you've never secretly desired men? What are the first names of the two feminist musicians Trull and Higbie?" I also become suspicious that my successful Lesbian friends will find out, and so I go to extremes to hide my problem. When I know women friends are coming over I make sure to break out the 900 feet of plastic ivy and drape it realistically around the front walk, then I line the lower balcony with my artificial heather, and dash to Safeway for a bundle of fifty-nine cent assorted tropical foliage for indoors.

It's not like I don't care about the little plants, either. I always try and make their time here with me as comfortable as possible, I even grind up little bits of Tylenol 3 and add it to their morning cup of coffee—but no matter how nice I am, throwing little wine tasting parties for them late at night and giving them lemonade and iced tea in the summer, they always die within a couple weeks. I've tried talking to them, letting them watch TV. I even thought they would like listening to music and so I went out and bought a Robert Plant album, but it never seems to matter. They always die within a couple of weeks and then there's the expense of the funeral.

Now it's spring again and I have no idea what to do. The last plant I had at my house was a cactus and he was actually doing well for a while. Then I decided that we should broaden the honesty base of our relationship through some light psychotherapy. I'll never forget how he looked the day I decided to help him let down his defenses. Someone later told me that you are never supposed to pull those poky things out of a cactus. Well, how was I to know? And for that matter, maybe if being a real Lesbian means you have to understand plants... well, Bellevue and 3.2 children aren't that bad, just don't plant anything near my picket fence.

Happy Gardening!  The Barmaid.

# LOVE ME, LOVE MY CAT

Cats. The world is full of them. They come in all shapes, sizes and colors. There are as many kinds of cats as there are people. Only one thing remains consistent about cats: they are all treacherous.

Now I know as an upstanding gay woman the number one rule is that I am supposed to *LOVE* cats. Almost every lesbian has one or two or even seven. Cats are to gay women like cows are to Hindus.

Enter the problem. As a young gay woman I wanted to fit in with my community. I went out and got the short haircut, bought the Levi 501's and listened to Joan Armatrading. It all seemed under control until my first date. The woman was an absolute peach of a gal who invited me to her apartment for dinner—and to meet her cat. The cat was a long-toothed Siamese named Guido.

Guido hated my guts from the moment he set eyes on me.

"I always let Guido screen my dates," the woman said. "I really trust his judgment."

Guido just stared hatefully. I wondered where Guido hid the remains of the girls he didn't okay. Probably buried in the cat box, I deduced. After all, cats can be really resourceful when pushed.

My date excused herself to use the bathroom. This left me alone in the living room with Guido. He weighed at least sixteen pounds and had eyes like Charles Manson. I looked around the room for something to defend myself with as Guido calmly began to groom. As he lifted his front paw he smiled cruelly and began to clean a set of razor-sharp ginzu knives posing as claws. I scooted back further into the corner of the couch. He stood up, stretched, and began to slither toward me.

"Nice kitty," I begged to no avail. The Ninja killer dressed as a common house cat reached out and in one move turned me from a fairly confident young lesbian into a blond kitty scratching post.

"Hey, knock that off, you fu—"

"Oh, that just means he really likes you," my dinner companion cooed just in time to see her devious little feline jump into my lap like we were old friends. I wondered if I should get a tourniquet for my bloody shin. It would mean having to move the cat. I weighed it over and decided just to bleed to death.

"Let me get you some wine," the peach offered. She was gone to the kitchen before I could stop her. As soon as she was out of the room Guido got up on the back of the couch and began to eat my hair. When I tried to move, he grabbed my head with the ginzu claws and chewed faster. He must have gobbled down about a two-inch patch before Peach came back with the wine.

Suddenly he was fast asleep. I was not fooled. I scooted away from him so that he was barely over my left shoulder. Just then he began go have a coughing fit. I turned, wine glass in hand, just in time to see him rolf a great big hairball right into my wine. I stared down at my glass. The hairball was from my hair that he had just eaten moments ago.

I guess I became a little upset.

"Do you know what your cat has been doing!?" I screamed. "In one half hour this hideous monster has mutilated my legs, eaten my hair, and thrown up in my drink! Can't you control it?!"

I stood up and made a lunge for the cat. Looking back, I'm not sure what I would have done if I had caught it. Luckily, Peach intervened.

"It's obvious that you don't like cats," she pouted. "I've never met a lesbian who doesn't like cats. I don't think I could ever trust you. I'm sorry; I think you'd better go."

She handed me my coat and opened the door. Outside it was raining cats and dogs. No, it was only raining dogs. I walked home in depressed silence wondering how a cat could wreck my whole evening, my whole life even! Without a love of cats, I was doomed in the lesbian community! I had to think of something. Maybe a small dog dressed as a cat?

As I walked up the steps of my apartment, I noticed something kind of furry and white sitting on my doorstep, something that looked like a grossly overweight, small, furry....

"Hey, relax," his eyes seemed to say to me. "I don't like cats either. I just happen to resemble one. Trust me; I think I have your problem solved."

I was mesmerized. The cat was all white, as big as a raccoon, and had one blue and one green eye. Almost as if I had no power of my own, I invited him in for some food.

It's been that way ever since. I guess I am a real lesbian now. When people come over they can meet not only one cat, but three. He eventually brought friends. Yes, I look like a full-fleged lesbian cat owner to all appearances. But just between you and me, the joke's on the girls who come over—he does a few typical kitty things and then disappears. He also makes the other ones do the same.

And when we're alone? Well, he likes to kick back and have a beer, and watch a good football game. That's my kind of a cat. There's only one rule: *Never* call him kitty.

# THE TROUBLE WITH BEING SWIMWEAR

The sun has never been my friend. It signals that special time of year when lads and lasses, responding to some primitive urge within, make themselves naked except for some ritualistic pieces of cloth that they call swim wear.

What I want to know is, who came up with today's swim wear? Who was the wise guy that said, "Let's show as much of our tanned, slim Adonis-like bodies as possible"—regardless of the fact that the ol' Barmaid stays as white as the moon, not to mention the lasagna-in-storage she's sporting. Every year it happens. Every year I try to make the best of it.

And then there's people like PicNic. PicNic owns a year-around tanning pass to any salon within the continental U.S. He also bought a clause to include Alaska, just in case. Besides his avid interest in tanning, PicNic's hobbies include weight lifting, swimsuit shopping and more swimsuit shopping. He is the only person I know that has bought a swimsuit from Gumps, Nehman Marcus, I Magnins, The Bon and Perry Ellis' estate all on the same day.

It wouldn't bother me so much if PicNic weren't such a dear friend and (yes, it's true) my beach buddy. I myself think that too much importance is placed on showmanship of the human body. After all, do any of us really like the way those bathing suits look when you try them on at the store? I always hate the underwear line I see when I look in the mirror (we all follow the rules, now don't we?), and then after hours of careful, frustrating shopping, you pick the suit that is you. Unfortunately. Swimsuits aren't like any other piece of clothing. Picking a bad suit is not like accidentally wearing a clashing shirt and tie. If you happen to purchase unflattering beach attire, it soon becomes apparent.

I once made the dreadful mistake of buying an all cotton bathing suit in pastel stripes. At the time I didn't realize that it did nothing for me and everything against me. As a matter of fact, no one said anything till summer was nearly over. One night when I was out with PicNic after another day at the beach, and I overheard him describing my bathing suit to some total stranger. "Rumba pants" and "A four year old in diapers" were two choice phrases I picked up, but the one that really ticked me off was "Slingshot". Hmmmmm.

I wondered if I should be a good friend and tell him that everyone at Madison Beach had nicknamed his bright orange terrycloth briefs the "Safety Trunks" or that the swim suit he had bought from Gumps actually clashed with the presentation bowl instead of matching it. Besides, only a real weirdo brings a presentation bowl to the beach. I decided not to tell him about the trunks or the fact that the Selsun blue didn't make those little white spots go away. If he wanted to be petty for humor's sake, he could do that, but I was going to have a little more restraint.

That was two years ago, and it was even worse last year. But this year, I got smart. I may have to get a new bathing suit because the "old one has a hole in the knee—har, har." Or maybe I'll take PicNic's other advice and "Wear the Anita Bryant special—you know, the one with the oranges already sewn in, har-har." And maybe, like PicNic says, I am "Soooo white that I make the queen feel black, Har-har." But I'll tell you one thing: there is such a thing as revenge. This winter and spring, I've had PicNic over to dinner 52 times. Lasagna. This year, when he orders his fabulous swim trunks, they're going to have to be from *Architectural Digest.*

# DON'T LET YOUR CHILDREN GROW UP TO BE COWPOKES

Yippie kai-yai Yo! It's your ever lovin' shit kickin' boot stompin' Barmaid writin' one hell of an article about them hot diggity, brush stompin', stump trainin' gay cowpokes.

Sound a bit fake? Pity. This particular Barmaid does not have an affinity for the western set. It's not that I don't like cowboys, it's just that I've never really made myself available to that particular subculture since my childhood.

I take that back, I did see a gay western musical once. It was called "Oklahomosexual", and it featured songs such as 'I'm Just a Guy Who Can't Say No,' 'Sorry, But the Fringe is on the Top', 'Firemen and Cowpokes ', 'Lesbee Friends', 'Oh, What a  Beautiful Myrna', etc. The musical wasn't that great, but the costuming was truly Divine (God rest her soul).

Anyhow, after that particular musical, the less I heard about rump rangers the better. I myself haven't seen that many prairie skirts since the Utah pioneer day parade, and I'm pretty sure even the Donner party would have passed on that particular cast.

Anyhow, since then I haven't done much dealing with the ol' western set till recently.  Recently is when it became a fashion statement to wear those snap-on shirts with the mother-of-pearl button snaps. Also the bolo tie rage, and—lest we forget—the biggest gay fashion trend of all—Cowboy boots!!

Five years ago you couldn't get a self-respecting gay person into shark skin boots with alligator tips, and now not only do they have the footwear but the dance steps to go with it!

I guess maybe it was curiosity that killed the barmaid, or maybe I just have a round-about way of doing things. Nevertheless, when all my gay male friends began going to the Timberline to learn the Two-step, the Ten-step, and the Cotton-eyed Joe, I couldn't swallow my pride enough to ask 'PicNic' and 'Fife' to take me, so I decided I'd show them...I'd learn them somewhere else...yeah!

That was it! I'd go to a bar where no one would know me, where some unsuspecting soul would teach me all of these fabulous dances, and then later—when I was the Ginger Rogers of the country set—I'd go back to the Timberline and wow the pants off my great buddies, PicNic and Fife.

It was on a Tuesday night when I first entered the Buckaroo Tavern. I had made a trip to Goodwill just hours before and picked up an authentic square dance skirt, the girl had assured me. I had also rented the movie "Urban Cowboy" to see for myself how straight cowgirls are supposed to act. I was only interested in how to get free dancing lessons, but once the movie started I didn't think that mechanical bull was such a bad idea either.

So here I was all dolled up in my hooped square dance skirt, red with black organdy ruffles, a black-ruffled western shirt with mother of pearl buttons and some really hot damn boots that I'd found for seven dollars at Jack Stallion's House of Used Highways.

I was especially proud of those boots. Red they were, with a naked lady riding a Brahma bull embroidered on the front. I felt confident of my dancing abilities in those boots. I was gonnna make that naked lady tow the ten-second bell and then some!

The first thing I did when I entered the bar was order a beer. I looked around. It wasn't that bad—why I had seen worse at Sappho's on an occasional night or two. I tried to keep in mind it would not set well with these "Cowboy's" if they saw me mentally undressing their girlfriends with my eyes. At that point I'm sure the girls wouldn't have been impressed either, considering my stunning outfit and as an added touch my lovely hairdo, which I had thought of myself. It was a Blonde Bingo style beehive with a little ringlet tail that was glued on with Bondo.

Bondo is an amazing glue that if put onto a bare patch of skin can render you sterile in minutes.

Well, needless to say, in that stunning outfit it took me no time at all to pick up the Mr. Goodbar of the Buckaroo. He was tall, and I use the term loosely, abut 6'7", with red hair, freckles, a red bandana and a checkered shirt. He reminded me of someone, someone I'd seen before, maybe at a party or some art show opening...it seemed like it was an event where a lot of prestigious people were present. Okay, maybe a good night at Mike's Lounge.

Anyway, whoever he was, I couldn't complain because he was, in fact, the only person who would talk to me in the ridiculous get up I had on. Oh, did I bother to tell you that all the other people (whom I believed to be goat ropers) were dressed in normal clothing and were just hanging out hoping to have a good time????!! I hated them. Hated them all except 'Goodbar'. He was serious about his art.

This wasn't just dancing: this was his life!

We danced the light fantastic and everything was fine until he told me I reminded him of Suzie.

"Suzie?" I screamed over the Patsy Cline song which was wailing in my ear.

"She was a horse I had when I was but a boy back on the farm, best stump broke pony I ever had!" He started to rub his hand up and down my organdy and suddenly I was reminded of what terminology "stump-broke" referred to.

"Hey mister," I said as I pushed him away roughly. "I don't know what you're thinking, but I assure you I have never been stump-broke nor do I intend to be."

"Well," he said smiling. "Perhaps the mechanical bull is more your trip." As he said this, he made a disgusting undulating gesture with his hips. I was at a loss for words. All I could think of was an expression I had heard at the gay bar frequently and before I knew it, out it came.

"Suck my dick!!" I screamed and ran for the door.

As I got in my car, a Mustang I might add, it finally dawned on me who the man resembled. I had been sexually propositioned by Howdy-Doody.

Later, down at the Timberline, I finally relaxed from the torrent of rage I had felt earlier. Back in my Levi's the world did not seem so grim: I had learned to Two-step, and being propositioned by Howdy-Doody wasn't that bad. After all, it could have been Clarabell.

# FONDUE FOOTBALL
## Or, Somewhere Over The Goalpost

The year that San Francisco went to the Superbowl I knew nothing about football. I didn't know a field goal from a tight end, a touchdown from a basket and knee pads from knee socks. I thought that Chuck Knox was a used car dealer and that Dave Krieg was the guy who ran that Nazi extremist group on Whidbey Island. I thought the Chicago Bears were a circus act and the Broncos were wild horses. When my lover, Madame X, asked me how I felt the Dolphins would do this year, I replied, "Okay, I guess as long as Greenpeace keeps up their efforts." At that point Madame X and my roommate, Saint, decided I needed some football knowledge, and fast. Hence it became their quest to turn Bouncy Barmaid into Burly Butch.

Now I am not a sports fan. As a matter of fact, I have spent the better part of my life avoiding any type of activity involving the so-called 'team sport'. In high school, I could be spotted doing the 50 yard dash past the P.E. area. And basketball was a dirty word. Once at a barbecue I accidentally agreed to play a friendly game of softball. The first time the ball was thrown my way, I was so frightened I spilled my cocktail, dropped my cigarette and broke a heel running to the nearest shopping mall I could find. It was at that point I came to the realization that I didn't care for sports.

As if sports in real life weren't bad enough, sports had invaded television. Television is supposed to be a fantasy place to escape to, it was not meant to be invaded by a bunch of grown men in matching outfits. The worst offender of this is football. It is a macho, aggressive, boring sport that only men drinking beer in their underwear watch. So what if I didn't understand it. I knew I hated it and would never watch it. What I didn't know was that I was living with die-hard

Football Lesbians!!!

When Madame X expressed her embarrassment at my ignorance about football, I didn't care much. Even an offer from Saint to do the dishes for a month if I'd learn the football basics didn't sway me. However, when Madame X promised me a trip to San Francisco during Superbowl week if I'd at least try, how could I refuse? San Francisco, the Gay mecca. I'd never even passed through San Francisco let alone spent a week there, and so I vowed to try.

Sunday after Sunday I sat in front of the T.V. Special football-watching Coaches were shipped in to help train me. My good friend, Prince, taught me that it was 'half-time' *not* 'intermission', and Dimples showed me how to serve beer and chips instead of wine and fondue. Madame X gave during-the-week instruction on the difference between the quarterback and the running back and why the players wore helmets and shoulder pads, and our friend, The Doctor, eventually broke me of wincing every time someone got hit. Little by little I became more confident with the game.

I learned to grunt, yell and slap my leg. When I finally achieved the ability to tell the teams apart Madame X decided I would go with her to the Superbowl town. The big S.F. !!!

I was so excited I could barely stand it. We would be in San Francisco for one whole week. Yes the Superbowl was on Sunday and we were going to a big Superbowl party with all of Madame X's football-watching friends, but that was only one day. The rest of the time would be sightseeing, shopping and socializing. Three of *my* favorite sports. I couldn't wait.

The week went by too quickly. It had been a glorious week and one I did not want to end, but, alas, it was Superbowl Sunday and our last day there.

The day was crisp and sunny and I was having a hard time thinking about spending four hours watching a stupid football game. But I had promised Madame X that I wouldn't embarrass her and I was determined to do my best. The women we were staying with were even tougher football freaks than I had imagined possible. They had 49ers T-shirts, mugs, and even the baby had a teeny, tiny football.

The minute the game started there was no frivolous chit chat. These girls were so serious about their football they even drank beer quietly, only cheering, swearing or making comments when the game warranted it. I was nervous. Quarter by quarter the game dragged on while I cheered, groaned and commented with the best of them. Finally at half-time, Mama Bear, Madame X's best friend for years, commented.

"You know Barmaid, none of us pegged you for the football type. We took bets that you didn't know knee pads from knee socks. I guess because you look so foofey, but you really know your stuff."

I looked over at Madame X. She was beaming. I smiled a huge smile and began to relax. Now that I was relaxing, the beer I was drinking tasted great. The time seemed to be moving faster and my mind kind of wandered back to Jr. High School. I wasn't so hopeless. I must have liked sports at one time because I remembered trying out for cheerleading in the eighth grade. Of course I didn't make it. But I could still remember the cheerleading moves we were taught to try out with. In order to try out, you had to do the splits. As I sat watching the game, I wondered to myself if I could still do those splits.

Maybe I should have eaten something that morning. Maybe I shouldn't have drunk so fast. I'm not sure what went wrong, but suddenly, before I knew it I was standing in the middle of the room doing a spur of the moment cheer.

I hadn't planned to block the T.V for the final touchdown. I hadn't planned to knock over the coffee table or throw up on the cat. On the drive home all Madame X would say to me was that we would never go back to California again.

Apparently my cheer left something to be desired—

"Knit one, pearl two
"Football Dykes, Yoo hoo!!"

117

# WHAT I DID LAST SUMMER

Well, boys and girls, winter is nigh.

No more basking in those glorious rays of summer sun. No more lying out on hot sweaty beaches, or slipping on a pair of those ultra-fashionable Jammies to drive in your stylish summer car (with the top down, of course) to your favorite bar, to sip cool cocktails and watch the sun set through the smoke-streaked windows.

Yes, it's true—winter is upon us. Hopefully.

What's this? Do I hear snorts of indignation? Sighs of regret?

Hold on, happy campers! Before I'm met with cries of outrage at my obvious pleasure in the return of Old Man Winter, let's talk about some of the overlooked, "finer" points of summer.

It started around May this year, if my memory serves me. One day we all awakened to—Ho! What's this? Sun! *Hot* sun! Egads! I felt like an old vampire who had been caught off guard. I remember running around my room throwing sweaters into storage, screaming, "The sun! The sun!"

There had been no time to prepare. Searching madly, I came up with an old pair of shorts from last summer, back when Hawaiian flower prints were in.

Oh, well—I could hit Nordstrom's later in the day.

Slipping on the shorts, I realized I wouldn't be hitting the same size rack as last year. I hadn't lost my winter squirrel fat. There I stood, Plumerias as big as horses across my butt and thighs. Then I noticed another dismal fact: the tree trunks that had once been my legs were sporting some awfully white bark.

I did a slow 360 in my full-length mirror and realized that *Sports Illustrated,* again this year, would be passing me up for their swimsuit edition.

Fat, white—and where the hell had my muscle tone gone? (Surely

119

you maintain *some* muscle tone watching TV. I myself move around a heck of a lot on that couch. And what about all those trips to the kitchen and bathroom? Don't they count for anything?)

I braved it and drove to the nearest cocktail lounge, to see if anyone else had been caught off guard. At least it would be dark there. *Very* dark, I hoped.

As I stepped into the ol' Cantina, I knew I hadn't been the only one unprepared for summer's sneak attack: it looked like a Fat Vampires from Hawaii convention in there.

Secretly I was pleased, but I knew I had to spring into action. It was summer! The pressure was on!

First, that call to the nearest tanning booth.

"Hello, Quick and Crispy Tan Salon?...Yes, I'd like to make an appointment. Well, several, actually. What color am I now? Probably the same color as Elmer's Glue...*I know it sounds serious, it is serious! Do you know the sun is out right now as we speak?!*...I'm sorry. Yes, it was rude. Yes, I do have an analyst...Whenever you can fit me in would be fine. *Next Tuesday!?*" Slam.

This was the first of the many fun things I love about summer.

Since I wasn't going to have any luck with the tanning booths today, I decided, as an alternative, to take care of the body mass. I'd just have to call the tanning salon back tomorrow under an assumed name.

My next stop was the Body Shop. Located in an alley entrance, it doesn't get much foot traffic, so there's always room for one more participant. I like it because they have all ex-Nazis for instructors, so for people like me who have a tendency to slack off or cheat, they have methods for keeping up the old heart rate.

As I approached the alley, I noticed a large congregation milling around the entrance to my secret workout haven. Word had gotten out, and everybody and their sister was there to sign up. Of course by the time they reached me, the classes were all full.

They would, however, have an opening in early October.

The only thing left to do was to go down to Nordy's and see about some summer camouflage wear to hide my current body shape. Maybe I could pick up a not-too-revealing swimsuit while I was there. It was worth a try.

I fought my way through the crowds of panicked summer shoppers and approached the now-empty racks. (I really do hate summer.)

Hanging on the swimsuit rack was one lone suit that had obviously been over-looked. Wait a minute! What a find! This suit was perfect! I held it up to my body and it looked like the perfect size. It was totally shapeless, but at this point, so was I.

Shoving the angry shoppers out of the way, I grabbed for the salesgirl and screamed, "I want a dressing room and I want it now!" The salesgirl looked at me like I was nuts, but she consented. I was led into a nice quiet room with a three-way mirror. Just what I needed.

"Remember to leave on your underthings," she chirped, as if I didn't know the rules.

I have long believed that the major department stores have made this underwear rule to con the average buyer into purchasing a bathing suit that looks like shit.

"Well, it will look better once you get it home and don't have those unsightly underwear lines showing," they always reason.

I myself didn't have to worry about unsightly underwear lines this time, because when I tried to put the damn suit on, I found it had no leg holes.

Now I was really mad. I knew I had a whole summer to go, and I wasn't going to take it. I marched out of the dressing room, ill-made swimsuit in hand, and in front of a whole line of frustrated shoppers screamed: "What is the meaning of this? All year long we support your store. We buy, buy, buy even when we have no money left to buy. Our closets are full of Nordy's this and Nordy's that: pants that show our socks, shirts that look like potato sacks, and we do it in the name of fashion! This time, however, you have gone too far! If you expect the people of Seattle to wear swimsuits with no leg holes, you are sadly mistaken! I am here to tell you this is not a fashion statement, this is a mistake!"

And with that, the crowd of angry shoppers began to cheer. They cheered right up until the time that the salesgirl said, in her most perfect salesgirl voice, "I'm sorry, ma'am, but what you've got is the bag for putting the swimwear in. It's not the suit itself—that's already sold out. I wanted to say something when you asked to try the bag on, but people go kind of crazy the first day of summer weather, and we've been instructed not to upset anyone."

"The bag?" I said.

"The bag," she confirmed.

"I knew that," I snapped. "I was just kidding around."

By now everyone was laughing. I even heard some fat little ten-year-old scream "What a dolt!" as I was leaving the store.

I'd love to say the summer went better after that, but after three months of salads, suntan oil, moisturizer, sun block, Nose Kote, hair lightener, beach parties, barbecues, charcoal in your teeth, camping, shaving, burning, peeling, bugs, and $2,000 worth of weight lifting equipment, I can't say I'll miss it.

I survived another summer and that's enough for me.

Now my semi-tan, fairly thin and in-shape body deserves a rest. I've already staked out my season position on the couch. It's a great place, close to the kitchen and bathroom, and directly under the skylight so I can frequently gaze up and watch the rain clouds roll by.

# 99 BOTTLES OF BEER

Someone recently asked me if I was really a Barmaid. Someone else recently asked me what a Barmaid was, and finally someone just two days ago saw me collecting a tip from a customer and yelled at the top of her lungs, "God! what an easy way to make money!!!" This is for all of you out there wondering and especially for all of you out there working in this 'biz— a tour of the bar. AND YOU ARE THERE.

6:55 p.m. on a Tuesday and we have just had a horrible fight with our beloved. The cat is at the vet's. The car broke down this morning and the workers at the house are two weeks behind. Waiting at home is about 30lbs. of unwashed laundry and an equal weight of unwashed dishes. We have on dirty socks but probably no one will notice because it is dark where we are rushing. We are rushing into a bar. We can see that about 50 other people have had the same idea but we will not be visiting them tonight. No, tonight we will be serving them. We are a barmaid.

7:00 p.m. We enter and smile at our Bartender 'Parker'. He grimaces back. "Full moon." he warns, and we turn in horror to see what is already going down in our work place. The crowd is not tame tonight. They are hot, they are tired, and most of them have one single purpose in mind. To get as intoxicated as humanly possible. It's going to be a fun night, we calculate.

We take a tray and begin the preliminary sweep of the bar. To the outside world this looks like cleaning the tables and picking up ashtrays and glasses. We are a barmaid. We know different. This time is assessment time. Who's out there, who are they with, what are they drinking, how much have they drunk, do they have car keys lying out on the table? Are they awake? Are they here to have fun, fix a bad mood, new in town or do they have a problem and need a friend as badly as a drink? We prioritize. We talk to those who look like they

123

need a friend. Why? Because we are not just a cocktail waitress, we are a barmaid. We care. We remember the names, the faces, the histories. And they remember us. As a barmaid we know they can go anywhere to drink. They choose here, partly because they know we remember and appreciate them, partly because today is ninety-nine cent drink day.

7:20 p.m. It's going to be a rough one. The 'Organ Grinder' is already here buying every cute guy in the bar a drink, and, as usual, his discriptions are less than informative.

"Hey, Barmaid, take that really cute guy a drink on me. I mean as long as it's a ninety-nine cent drink." We look around. Which guy? We figure he means the guy over there drinking a screwdriver so we go up to Parker and order.

"Order in!"

Two drunk guys at the bar respond, "Blow it out your ass!" We are happy to see that they both have coffee in front of them. We run the Screw to the guy that the 'Organ Grinder' pointed to, and just as we hand him the drink and explain the circumstances the 'Organ Grinder' stands up on a chair and yells across the crowd, "Not him!!" We grab the screwdriver and hand it to the other guy who is, of course, drinking a rum and coke.

"Here hon, you look like you could use some vitamin C," we say winking. "It's from the 'Organ grinder'."

He groans. Everyone in the city knows the 'Organ grinder'." We go back to the 'Grinder.'

"Could you do that one more time?" he asks, "You see that cute guy over there..." He hands us a quarter. It's going to be a long night.

8:30 p.m. Shit. Shit. Shit. That same group of straight kids that always comes in just came in. We have a hard time with them; they tend to give us a headache where we sit. Usually they don't come in until later, which is good because they are so loud and obnoxious that they tend to drive off our good customers and our good tippers.

"Hey babe," the 23 year old God's gift to women says to us, "I'll buy if you fly."

We barely hear him however because we are watching Ricardo Hernandez-Jones stand up on a bar stool and scream into the crowd, "Help!!! I need a man!!!" This could prove to be disastrous. People on barstools have incited whole wave reaction riots before, we know, we've seen them. This situation must be stopped at once but with kid gloves.

"It sounds like a job for the Barmaid," we jeer, humming the Mission Impossible theme song.

We calmly walk over to him, and full of force we say "Ric, don't need a man, be one. Get down off of that stool and have some sense." His friends laugh and cheer as Ric sheepishly dismounts.

"Hey babe! How about that round?"

We know without turning around that it is 'The Gift'. We don't go back to his table. We know already what he wants. As a matter of fact we usually know what every person in the bar drinks. His table is particularly fond of Tequila shooters and Electric Iced Teas. Parker is paying attention to the vocals in the bar and has set up the order practically before we get there. Just as we are about to leave the service area we get stopped by Don and Jon and their fabulous cat pictures.

"Oh, my, look at how much Missy has grown since last Tuesday," we remark. It is the same thing we have remarked for the last 50 Tuesdays. They both smile that twin-lovers smile and are pleased that we noticed. What the heck, it's probably the only child they're planning on having—of course they're proud papas. We start to tell them what wonderful parents they are when suddenly we can hear with our Barmaid's sixth sense some trouble brewing... let's see, a fight... aggressive energy coming from... hummm... uhuh... over there! Right on target! Just as we pinpointed the hot spot, we see and hear old Bert the nurse raise his voice.

"Get out of my way you ugly sonofabitch!" We try to see over the sea of heads.

"I said MOVE IT!!" he yells menacingly.

We know Bert is just a few bricks short of a load sometimes, and we know that on those times he will pick a fight with just about anyone. We hope for our sakes it isn't a professional wrestler as we dash in to break it up. We wedge in between all the hot, drinking bodies and finally come to where old Bert seems to be challenging the other person.

"You are the ugliest, stupidest, sorriest excuse for AN ASSHOLE I have ever seen, and if you don't get out of my face I'm going to do something about it!!"

We look at his opponent and decide to let him handle this one himself. We wonder how long it will take Bert to figure out that he is talking to the mirror.

Somehow, as we were running to rescue Bert, we have managed to unload our tray of drinks at The Gift's table. He can see what a busy night it is, so in an unprecedented gesture, when we tell him the round of drinks is $24.75 he hands us .25 cents and says, "Keep the change." We can't believe it. What a guy!! And he has only tried to feel our crotch about three times tonight. Times are a changin'!

9:50 p.m. We wonder why we didn't take our mother's advice and become a doctor or marry one. The place is jammed. People forget that they have to work tomorrow or maybe it's just that they forget that we have to work ever again. Orders are flying faster than Cessnas. There is a line from the bar to Africa. We have three tiers of drinks stacked on our tray and then, in walk Rocky and Bullwinkle. We stop everything. We unload our tray and call Parker for an order.

"Scotch and milk, rum and coke."

Quickly we get over and deliver the drinks.

"Thanks Barmaid," they say, and then they say it louder with a tip.

They have learned that tipping talks. A lot of our clientele has learned that. It's not that we prioritize in this business, it's just that we tend to remember a dollar better. Understandable enough. And don't forget, the government is charging bar workers eight cents on every dollar whether we receive a tip or not. Of course we remember a dollar, it's what is paying our rent!!

11:20 p.m. We wished we had bought new shoes. We wonder how much longer our knees are going to hold up. We want to know why that little blond man at the end of the bar is making faces to himself. Parker is starting to get punchy. Now we are having some fun. If it were slower we'd make toilet paper hats for the good customers. The good customers say thank god it isn't slower.

The guy with the Seahawks hat comes in just like usual.

"You probably don't remember me," he starts out.

"But I gave you a fifty cent tip once!!" the whole bar has joined him in unison.

"Yes, we remember you," we say. We want to tell him we spent it wisely, we think we phoned a cab and ordered a pizza. By this time of night traditionally, we at the bar take a fatality count. We count how many times we were knocked over, (for us that was 7), stepped on (12), pushed (500), picked up and thrown around (here the littler you are, the higher the count – we always win this category! 17) and last but not least, the strangest case of mistaken identity. We almost won tonight because a guy that came up from Sonja's thought we were a girl he met in the war who's name was Esmirelda, but then at the last moment, Parker told the same story. This is also the mandatory time to say what a scary night it's been. Now we settle in for the last rush, sometimes known as "Weirdo's Rush".

1:55 a.m. This is it, the end of our evening. Now we just need to get the die-hards out so we can clean up and get out ourselves.

"Free buffet at Thumpers if you get there before two!" yells Parker. About seven people run out the door.

"Also an open bar!" he adds and another fifteen people leave. We see this guy slip a drink into his overcoat and start to walk out the door.

"Hey," we tease as we stop him gently, "Let's see what you've got in there, you better give it to us."

He opens his overcoat and inside he has his drink but nothing else. He wags his wiener at us and laughs. We look him up and down sarcastically.

"If you're planning on drinking that drink this year, your going to need a bigger straw than that," we sneer.

The man is chagrined. He discretely buttons up his overcoat and then smiles.

"Three points," he winks.

"Get home safely," we counter with a smile. When he leaves, we lock the door screaming "Quick! Lock the door!!"

It's a weird job. An even weirder career, but we suppose someone has to do it. We count our sixty or seventy dollars in tips, wonder if our right foot will need x-rays and kiss Parker good-night. "What an easy way to make money!" echoes in our head. Damn straight, we think sarcastically, sure would hate to have a hard job like, oh, say at a bookstore.

# EDDIE'S O'GILL

I had worked at this one Gay men's bar called Big Eddie's for two years and had become familiar with the regular clientele that inhabited it. A very friendly group they were, who, for the most part, drank well, tipped well and all got along well. The weekday evening Bartender, 'PicNic' was a gentle man with a quick sense of humor and (so I'd been told) "a body to die for." I, the Barmaid, was known to everyone as 'Melba Toast'. All winter we had enjoyed each other's company, and even though the bar was located in a possibly rough part of town, no one had taken out exorbitant life insurance policies—nobody that is until the spring of '86.

The first time was probably just bad luck. A strange man had come into the bar, ordered a drink, and then proceeded to boast about how he'd just demolished a "Fairy" bar in Alaska. The group at the bar, all men, immediately began talking about auto mechanics. This occasionally happens, I have noticed, when a small number of Gay men are confronted with an angry, drunk straight man big as an oak tree who is eating his glass after drinking the drink. The man left, but later we heard he had stumbled across another Gay bar and had started a fight with two men.

The second time was about three days later, and Big Eddie's was not so lucky. 'Our man Flint' was bartending, and the situation got so out of hand that the police had to assist. After that it became such a regular problem that a special staff meeting was called to advise the employees.

"I don't know how to explain what's going on," the manager began, "But we seem to be getting an abnormal number of dangerous people lately. Now, how to handle it...I don't know. Don't take any chances. Usually these guys don't know they're in a Gay bar, and when they find out, they get really mad!! I wish I knew of a way to handle this, but the best thing I can suggest is to call 911 and hope they hurry."

Although PicNic and I had not yet had a problem, we knew from the other Bartenders that 911 was not always fast enough. It was a scary thought and deep down in my little chicken heart I was praying for a new job.

I was still at Big Eddie's on St. Patrick's Day, my mother's favorite day of the year. At home, St. Pat's Day was almost as important a holiday as Easter. You see, Mom believes in Leprechauns, Gnomes and Faeries—"the old folk" she calls them, and she tells how they can look just like human beings all year round, but on St. Patty's day, "They show their magical powers and perform miracles the likes of which you've never seen."

I personally never believed my mother and as far as seeing any "human-looking" folk performing miracles on this day, the closest I've ever come, is seeing grown men consume their weight in green beer. I was seeing that "miracle" again this evening at Big Ed's. PicNic and I had been working our shaleighlies off all evening, and it had finally slowed down at about twenty to twelve. I was just sitting down at the bar, when suddenly this man came in. A very familiar-looking man but I couldn't place him. He ordered a drink, a double bourbon—no ice. He gulped it down and had a second. The man made me nervous. He had that killer look, and I knew he didn't run for Empress, I mean, with those looks, what would be his drag name? Ram-Bo Derek?

That was it, too!! The furtive glances around the bar, the tattoo on his arm of the atom bomb explosion, the bulge under his fatigues that looked like heavy artillery... Rambo! The guy was Rambo! I started talking about auto mechanics, and so, unfortunately, did Sofanda Peters.

"Hey, that broad sounds really weird!" growled Rambo.

"Girlfriend, you don't sound so pretty yourself!" Sophie answered.

"Hey, she's not a she, she's a he!" the man calculated. He took another look around the bar noticing men sitting with men and me talking about the children. Suddenly, he straightened up and said, "You're a bunch of F——ing Queers!!" No one moved.

"I'm gonna bash some heads in 'cause you're all a bunch of F—ing Queers aren't ya?" Still no one moved.

I'm not quite sure what happened next for I have never believed in the St. Patrick's day "miracles of the human-looking folk," but suddenly the man stood up (I could see he was going to kill us all) and focused his attention on PicNic who was only six inches away.

"Hey Bartender, this is a F—ing Fairy bar and you're all a bunch of F—ing Fairies, aren't you?!! Say it!!"

PicNic looked him straight in the eye for a long moment. I felt a slight breeze from nowhere in particular rustle my shirt, and a voice from somewhere beyond PicNic's boomed, "YES WE ARE ALL FAIRIES AND WE HAVE MAGICAL POWERS, SO BE GONE!!!"

The whole bar was mesmerized. I turned to look at the man but he had disappeared, artillery and all!!

Later, after the bar had closed I asked PicNic how he had done it.

"I'm a fairy," he replied matter-of-factly.

"What do you mean you're a fairy?" I asked sarcastically.

"I am." He stated again, "I read it on a coffee cup. It said Fairy, Faerie: An imaginary being of romance and folklore, usually possessing magical powers, and 12 Lacoste shirts in assorted colors."

# A LETTER TO
# THE GANG AT WORK

I work at a little bar on 15th and Madison in Seattle, but basically this bar could be any bar, any bar in any town, and it probably is.

Did I say any bar in any town? Well, that's almost true. I meant any gay bar in any gay town.

That's the difference—and it is a difference.

I remember the six months I worked in Ballard. I was bartending at that time, my clientele consisting of about 20 huge men who could drink 75 drinks and still be standing (but not well). Actually, 19 men could still be standing. Old Mel had his right leg cut off after a logging accident, and he didn't exactly stand after 75 drinks. Of course he gave it one hell of a try though—forgot all about the fact that he'd unstrapped his wooden leg at the start of the day, and along about five o'clock he'd stand up to leave.

For some weird reason, I'd always be somewhere too close to old Mel when he decided to get up. So I ended up underneath him about once a week. That always inspired a big razzing from the other 19 men, who all worked either on fishing rigs or in logging camps.

It wasn't because of the guys that I left that job and ran to a gay bar job. No, it was more in the interest of world peace. See, I didn't really feel comfortable with the fact that they thought my lover at the time was a guy, especially since she used to sit right there at the bar with them and they couldn't even tell.

It was like the idea was so unfathomable that they would rather just assume that she was a young man with a fairly high voice who knew a lot about auto parts. I remember this one time a man I fondly refer to as Guido asked me, "Why do you have such a feminine boyfriend?

Wouldn't you rather have a real man?"

Boy, Guido didn't know what he'd actually said, and I wasn't about to stick around there until he put it together. That's when I left the ol' gin bar of Ballard and hiked it up to the hill to be with my own kind: gay men.

Gay men?

Yes, Gay men. Those crazy, crazy guys who know more about fashion than Gloria Vanderbilt. Those silly guys who scream "Sister, Mother and Girlfriend" to almost anyone that walks through the door. Those fun-loving guys who drink such drinks as Fannybangers and Blowjobs like they are water, dancing and singing at the top of their lungs, screaming and cursing when the lights go up at last call and clapping and cheering every time Charles Pierce or Diana Ross comes up on the video screen.

Granted, I occasionally have to pick someone up off the floor when a cagey bar stool has somehow eluded their weaving buttocks... I still have an occasional fight to break up (mostly just a pull-hair-and-nail fight) and every so often someone will ask me if I don't want to date a real man.

They are usually referring to their sister, but it's just not the same. Here, the people who come in soon grow to be family, and—like family—it's for better or for worse.

In all honesty, I have to say it's mostly better, and the "worse" gets taken care of right away. I don't really mind the times you guys feel the need to table top dance, or when you try to hide in the bathroom to avoid leaving at last call.

I understand the moody days and all about male P.M.S. now, and have familiarized myself with the gay man family tree (it looks similar to a privet hedge as far as I can figure).

And, you? Why you have all learned to tolerate and—low and behold—have almost come to love me despite my changing hairdoes, my female P.M.S., and the education I insist on giving you about the gay women's culture and natural habitat.

We truly have a symbiotic relationship, you and I. I serve you well while you are here, and you help me make my house payment.

Okay, enough bullshit.

It's not just the job. We're friends—dear friends some of us—and that isn't weighed in straight or gay employment benefits. I love you guys, and, because of that, I enjoy my work.

It makes me happy, and I hope I return the favor.

# A LETTER HOME

Dear Mom,

I am writing to you on behalf of every person who wants to write their mother a letter.

When I think of you, Mom, many things go through my head. I try to define your role in my life and I just never seem clear on what your "occupation" really is.

You are a wonderful gal and have many talents. I still can't figure out how it is that you can take a mixture of outfits from K-mart and I. Magnin's and pull it together enough to wear in public.

Among your other mysteries is the way in which you can make gravy with no lumps, your own doughnuts from scratch and make minute pieces of paper hold so many coherent phone messages.

You have an uncanny knack for knowing every character in every soap opera, and the ability to keep what you wear to bed such a secret that sometimes I wonder if Dad even knows.

Always a lady, I have heard you say 'marvelous' and make it convey 'bullshit', and 'really' to 'who gives a rat's ass?' without batting an eyelash. You have entertained flawlessly some of the most boring people on the face of the earth, and have done it so well that no one even knows about the half empty bottle of NO-DOZ in the kitchen.

You have lost incredible battles, only to emerge victorious in the war.

Remember when I was 14, I screamed "no more Toni home perms!! No more home perms ever!!" You smiled and walked away, only to watch me ten years later pay $60 a trip for the same thing—my own decision.

Yes, you are a psychic.

One of my favorite demonstrations of your abilities is the uncanny way you seem to know when I am in the midst of a romantic interlude, and you call "just to chat." Of course I can't even take the phone off the hook because you drilled into me the fact that it might be some family disaster that only I could fix.

Pretty clever, Mom.

You like me in dresses; I visit you in Levis. You wish I'd gain weight; I diet and exercise frantically.

Some of the more amazing things you've told me in my life range from the fact that murderous killers hang out at the drive-in to the fact that there are werewolves in Woodenville, WA.

You always try to understand me, but just so I don't get a big head you take every opportunity to tell me you don't and that you wish I'd have a child just like me to worry and fret and stew about.

As a doctor you practice the strangest kind of medicine I've ever seen. Your remedies do seem to work, but how come they always begin with the advice "Quit Smoking"?

Other invaluable advice has included little gems like 'always wear clean underwear,' 'buy shoulderstrap handbags' and 'pretty is, as pretty does'. This last one took a long time to hit home Mom, but as usual you were right.

The thing about mothers is that even when they are wrong they are right— and I can't count the number of times I have fallen victim to your strange philosophy of life. Things do even out in the end—you are right—but I just can't be content to read *Reader's digest* and wait. I know you're laughing right now, you always laugh when I am young and impatient.

Mom, take it light when I say that mothers are the reason God created therapists. You had a mother too, you should know what I mean.

The bottom line is that somewhere inside all of us children, we love the mom in our mothers. You've embarrassed me, enlightened me, frustrated, comforted, and really done me in sometimes. Every mother on the face of the earth has a child to thank, don't forget. And I doubt that any of us will forget any of you.

Mom, I love you, and I'd do anything for you.

Except go straight.

# TRICK OR TREAT
# WHICH WITCH?

Why witches should be on my mind now, I have no idea. But there they are, bold as day, just sitting on the right side of my brain taking up creative space.

It's not the witches of my adult life either. Those happen to be nice, real women who have a certain spiritual belief system that I can appreciate.

No, this is more like the witches of my childhood—namely old Mother Witch.

In some families Santa Claus is a big deal. A big enough deal that someone's uncle Joe, every year, would trudge up the rickety attic steps late on Christmas Eve, get the old felt Santa suit that smelled of mothballs and scotch, and reappear several mothballs and scotches later careening around authentically on the roof.

"Look kids, there's Santa!" the dad would shout in mock surprise which sounded pretty authentic to the kids. Actually the surprise part **was** authentic because the dad really had no idea whatsoever that his drunken brother Joe would get on a steep roof like that after fifteen or so shots of the ol' Scotsman.

Then the kids would squeal, and Santa would look very surprised, like he had just been caught in a mischievous act. Thank God the kids did not see Santa urinating off of the back slope of the roof just moments before (even Santa has a small bladder after 15 or so Scotches).

That cheery little scene never happened in my family though. No, we had another sort of holiday personality that would visit us every year. Ours was a bit more awesome than some drunk uncle dancing around on the roof—and also a wee bit more embarrassing.

We had Mother Witch.

Mother Witch came into our family long before I was born, and there she decided to stay. Dressed in basic black, she was quite a frightening figure.

She resembled a cross between an ancient Transylvanian peasant woman and Freddie Kruger. She was also just as deadly to young trick-or-treaters, such as me and the myriad of cousins, nieces and nephews who ventured forth on All Hallows Eve hoping to score big in the chocolate department.

Mother Witch was a Sadist. She was also a close relative, although I did not find this out until well into my adult years.

It was very simple, in my family—no matter where you were or what you were doing, on Halloween you could count on a visit from Mother Witch.

The first time I ever remember seeing Mother Witch was when I was about six years old. I was out trick-or-treating with my evil cousin, Caren, and my brother, the Baseball, not to mention about six other nondescript cousins ranging from age eight on down. We were having a fine time, us kids, costumes attached, white pillowcases in hand.

Suddenly there was shriek of terror from the front of the line. We had just come upon a block in our neighborhood that was not well lit and a dead end to boot. Into the crisp night air, one of the oldest cousins gave a bloodcurdling scream. Needless to say, the rest of us followed suit just out of general principle, and the night was rent with the vocal terror of eight tiny persons.

At first, like most of my cousins, I had no idea what we were screaming about. But it seemed like a good idea.

Then I saw her. She was the ugliest apparition I had ever seen—and real. There was no pointy hat or hooked nose. There was no black cat or long stringy white hair. Oh, no. This wasn't a witch like in the movies. We had come up against the real thing—the thing we had been warned about and feared to see. The thing we wanted to avoid at all costs; Mother Witch!

All eight of us dropped our Halloween candy and ran. The Baseball even peed his pants.

Nobody blamed him, however. After all, Mother Witch was damned serious business.

She chased us forever but somehow we all got away—which was a good thing. Those poor, unfortunate children who didn't... well, we all knew what happened to them. Mother Witch would tie them to her broom and fly them to the nearest water tower which she called her cooker pot. There she'd boil them down into a fine soup and eat them up—even sucking the marrow out of their bones!

When I saw her gnarled hands clutching a very clean white bone, and gazed at her blackened, sharp teeth, I knew it was all true.

For years she followed us around. Even if we split up, somehow she'd find us. Lucky for us, though, all she ever caught was our bags of candy. This never seemed to matter because our own mother seemed to have a great stash of trick-or-treats after every Halloween.

Even after I became too old to trick-or-treat, this old witch would find me. Once at a high school dance. Once at a party. Once necking at some park with a boy who, when he saw her, ran away and left me in the car with no keys. Luckily she chased after him instead of me, and I just happened to run into my dad driving down the road home.

Why, she even showed up at my first lover's house one Halloween. We had decided to stay in and be romantic, though there was no romance after that little encounter. Trust me.

I had gone on assuming that Mother Witch really was a Witch or at least a crazy woman. After all, over the years this woman had been pissed on, hit in the head with a rock, grazed by a car, pushed down a hill, and feared and hated by all, what relative would subject her/himself to all this just to make Halloween a little more authentic?

I would have kept my views about Mother Witch being a total stranger—except for one thing. One Halloween when I was about 21, I got the job of taking my nieces and nephews trick-or-treating. Per usual, about a half-hour into the candy gathering, big as life, who should appear but Mother Witch!

Times had changed, however. People no longer took Mother Witch with a grain of salt. Before she could even say "I want to suck your sweet young bones," two college-age boys jumped out of nowhere and started hitting her with her own broom.

One boy gave her a punch in the eye, and the police were there almost immediately. They loaded her in to the squad car, and off she went to the pokey.

I took the kids home, then went to find my mom and dad to tell them the good news.

139

My mom wasn't home. She usually had things to do on Halloween. But my dad always stayed home to answer the door.

I recounted the story to him, and when I got to the part about her being hauled away in a police car, he completely flipped out.

"Geezus Christ shit! Now she's finally done it!" he was yelling, as he grabbed his car keys and headed out the door.

That's when it finally dawned on me.

My dad came home a couple of hours later with my mother sheepishly in tow. She had a fierce black eye, but I wasn't about to ask her how she got it.

As a matter of fact we never talked about that evening. And the next year, right on schedule, Mother Witch appeared, this time to hassle me at the gay bar. She's shown up every year after, but she's not moving quite as fast as she used to.

This year I can't seem to get her off my mind. I mean, with all the crazy stuff going on out in the world now, I just don't know if it's a safe place for a Halloween witch anymore.

If you see her this year, do me a favor and sort of be gentle with her. After all, she's like family to me.

# DESPISING
# THE RED MENACE

All year long I came from a fairly normal family. I, as a child, had the basic family package: strange relatives, a mom, a dad, a white picket fence, a little brother and other family pets... we even had a color TV.

Yes, it was pretty much the model family from January through October, but every year like clockwork came those other two months—the holiday months.

They say that the Ghouls come out on Halloween. I believe this is so. What they don't tell you, however, is that those Ghouls are disguised as people who know and love you. Your family, your relatives—all the grown-ups that you normally count on. The Ghouls take over your loved ones some time around 2:00 a.m. on November 1st.

It's always the Moms they go for first, then Aunts, Dads and even Grandmas.

I wouldn't have believed it myself except that, until I figured it out, I saw it happen every year. You go to bed on Halloween night after a profitable time trick-or-treating, your pillowcase loaded down with sugary goodies that you intend to live off for the next week, and you fall asleep, completely unaware of the evil that is about to stalk your house.

The next morning, hurriedly you dress and run to the kitchen to find your mother—surely she will call the police—as you round the corner, you stop dead in your tracks. There is your loving mother standing by the stove making ... hot breakfast? Something is very wrong.

Yes, it's your mother, but it appears that Stephen King has come in and performed a make-over on dear old Mom. You decide to try and communicate with the thing that used to be your mother. Innocently you ask this fiend with glinty red eyes and Medusa hair if she has seen your trick-or-treat candy.

"I hid it!" she screams and laughs wickedly, "And if you find it and eat it without permission, SANTA won't bring you any presents!"

Well, there it is. One by one all the adults you know are taken over by the Undead, and as the month progresses you can get a feel for who's behind this.

"SANTA sees everything!" "SANTA won't bring you anything if you don't...!" "Have you been a good little girl for SANTA?"

It became clear to me that this Santa guy had some bizzare control over adults and kids alike.

I wasn't crazy about the idea. You see, I learned to dislike Santa at a very early age. For one thing, I knew the guy had a pretty sadistic streak in him by the way he behaved at my house. He was always making value judgements based on gender, and it ticked me off.

Take my seventh Christmas for example: I get up in his pudgy lap and ask for a race car set. Everyone in the mall can see me and I am highly embarrassed; however, I know this is the only way to get the fat guy to deliver. Christmas morning I run out to the tree to find the race car set and there is one, all right—for my bald little brother.

I got a Barbie.

This continued every year, until finally the last straw was on my tenth Christmas, when I really needed a toolbox and I get—a cradle with a rubber doll that wets its pants.

That's when it hit me. My parents became these monsters every time this Santa guy showed up; all the adults I knew got pretty weird, and I was a nervous wreck. I put two and two together and realized this guy was not a "jolly old elf" but rather a leftover Nazi, hiding out in a beard and a red suit and determined to wreck the American family.

No wonder parents and grown-ups became so strange this time of year. They were being programmed by a fat guy in a felt suit.

It was then, in my eleventh Christmas, that I decided to speak out against Santa.

Thanksgiving that year was the same as usual for everyone except me. I knew the truth, and it made me see things differently. I now knew why Grandma overcooked the turkey, why there were onions the size of Pittsburgh in the giblet gravy, and why my grandfather once again made the speech to us kids about how we would look back on these days with the fondest of memories.

My mother, who was truly starting to look like one of the characters from Night of the Living Dead, just kept smiling and asking anyone who would listen if they had finished their Christmas shopping yet. She only stopped once, and that was when my Aunt Dot said to me, "Someday you'll have children and then you'll understand about holidays."

That is when my mother smiled knowingly, and I realized she took great pride in thinking soon she might say these frightening words to my children (boy did I fool her!)

Then my Uncle Lenny, who always came to Thanksgiving, Christmas and New Years dead drunk, stood up as the mashed potatoes were being passed and announced that his eldest daughter was a slut.

Then he said his wife was a slut and so was the dog.

My grandma disagreed with him about the dog and so did his older brother, my Uncle Bub. My Uncle Bub has always reminded me of a peach with eyes and a hat, and apparently my cousin thought so too, because she stood up and said she didn't need "no peach with a hat" defending her virtue.

No one had the heart to tell her that Uncle Bub was defending the dog, especially me. I knew my evil cousin Caren, I knew what she was capable of doing, even if she was only twelve. She may not have been a slut, but at eleven years old, I was pretty sure she had the capabilities of a mass murderer.

I decided to remain quiet, and would have if only my born-again cousin and her born-again husband hadn't decided to be so darned Christian and try to break up the fight with lively conversation.

The first rule in my family has always been when Grandma and Uncle Lenny get in a fight, you just let it go till Grandma punches him out. No mess, no hassle, and Grandma still feels useful.

Anyway, Cousin Tami had obviously been in one of those retreats too long because, out of the blue, she said, "So, little Barmaid, what do you want Santa to bring you this Christmas?"

If I had been expecting the question maybe I could have fielded it more diplomatically. As it was, completely unaware of the timing, I announced matter-of-factly, "I don't want anything from that old Nazi."

If I had waited even another ten seconds to answer, my grandmother probably would have made contact with Uncle Lenny, and Thanksgiving would have ended as usual. As it was, my statement threw her so off-balance that she missed him completely, sailed on through the fruit salad, over the credenza, and landed, crash! with a broken hip.

From that time on the family said I would never be any good.

Santa never delivered any more Christmas presents, which was okay with me—I mean who needs another Barbie doll anyway? And besides, after I gave up Santa I still got as many presents—still as weird, but they were all from Mom and Dad so they could be exchanged.

I don't know who told Santa about my discovery, but even to this day, when I walk through the shopping mall around Christmastime, I feel beady little eyes on me staring, penetrating. I turn and there he is, grimacing behind that beard.

I look at him, and I think of how much my mom and dad have changed since I dared to speak out. They are no longer the scary Ghouls of long ago. He stares at me a moment longer and tries to tell me with his eyes that it wasn't him, it was never him, it's just that I'm older now, and my parents have mellowed with age.

"Yeah," I whisper with *my* eyes, "Then bring me a toolbox."

# I'LL BE ꞪOꟽO FOR
# CꞪRISTꟽAS

Ho, Ho, Ho! It's that time of year again, and what that basically means to you and me is at least one mandatory visit to the family. No, I'm not talking the extended family—I mean your real family. The one you didn't pick. The one that has your fat Aunt Gert. The one where Uncle George is always asking who you're dating these days. And Cousin Les makes those extremely witty "gay" jokes all night long. Yes, it's the holiday season, complete with pumpkin pie, Grandma's walker, and the family closet.

I became thoroughly familiar with the family closet just a few years ago. It isn't like I went out of my way to hide my lifestyle, but when sitting next to my Uncle Lenny (a retired KKK devotee) the topic just never came up. Mom and Dad knew, of course. If you were perceptive, you could tell by the way they flinched every time we sang "don we now our gay apparel." But no one ever said anything about homosexuals. That is, however, until the Christmas Aunt Freida came to visit.

Aunt Freida was a distant relative whom no one had ever seen except in old photographs. She had been in Europe for as long as I had known, and when her name came up, the details were always sketchy at best. Then, about three years ago, we were all just sitting around bracing ourselves to hear about the time my grandfather was chased by the Christmas goose (for the fiftieth time). Suddenly, there was a very forceful knock at the door.

"Who is it?" my mother asked in her best holiday voice.

"Open the door! It's colder than a witch's tit out here!" the robust stranger bellowed. Before you could say "Tiny Tim," the door was pushed open and in stomped the most interesting woman I had ever seen.

"Frieda!" the older members of the family gasped in unison. "Frieda?" I questioned. So this was the infamous Aunt Freida! The goose story had obviously gone by the board (thank God), and instantly I got the distinct feeling that an episode of Dynasty was about to be filmed in my grandma's dining room.

"What are you doing here?!" my grandmother hissed. This was very strange. Grandmas aren't supposed to hiss. They bake cookies and take naps, but they do not hiss.

"Spreading holiday cheer, you old crack!" my aunt replied loudly. Loud was a great way to describe my aunt. At nearly six feet tall, with shorn salt and pepper hair, she looked quite capable of spreading anything she wanted to—including my Uncle Lenny (a decidedly interesting thought).

I knew at once that I liked Aunt Freida . Maybe it was the bomber jacket she had on. It was a real one—from the war I mean! It wasn't the kind of thing a lady of her years would normally wear, but then again she didn't seem "normal."

Suddenly I remembered a story—a little bit about Aunt Freida, something whispered between my mom and grandma when they thought I was sleeping: Didn't they say something about a female companion? Hmmm.

My grandmother's voice interrupted my train of thought. "We'll have none of your trashy talk or personal conquests discussed here Freida. Just you remember that if you intend to stay here for dinner. We are not interested in your personal life. Not one bit. Just remember that too!"

I looked at my Aunt Freida. I wasn't sure what had happened between her and my grandmother, but after all these years it couldn't be that important. This was a family member, one of the matriarchs of our clan, no matter what her sexual orientation. And it was Christmas!

It didn't take a genius to figure out what was going on, and it occurred to me that the very same thing could be happening to me in a few short years. I couldn't stand it. Maybe I had just been waiting for a catalyst—an excuse to stand up and be counted. Maybe I would have spilled the beans that Christmas anyway, I'm not sure. All I know was that something snapped inside of me that evening and in front of God and everyone I spoke my piece.

"Aunt Freida , are you gay?" I demanded.

"Well of course I am," she replied as though it was perfectly out in the open.

"Well, you needn't pretend that everyone is okay with that," I declared, my voice rising. "Frankly, I don't give a damn if you are or not, but I am ashamed at the way my family has always hidden you. Just because you have a different lifestyle, some members of this family have pretended that you didn't exist!"

"Please sit down, Barmaid," my mother said, tugging my arm.

"No I won't sit down, Mother. It's time this kind of behavior stopped. Not just here but everywhere. Just because Aunt Freida is gay we have written her out of the family. We don't talk about her because we don't want to upset Grandma, and then when she finally shows up no one even welcomes her. And you Grandma, I'm ashamed of you. I can't believe that you would treat a family member like this just because she has a different sexual preference. Well, you better just throw me out too, because I'm just like my aunt. Yes, Grandma, I've been with women!"

With every word, I felt more and more invigorated. My righteous indignation had my blood rushing with the energy of high drama. But for some reason none of the family had fainted or gasped. And after a speech like that! It was so disappointing.

After a pregnant silence my cousin clued me in. "We already knew about you, Barmaid," she whined in a bored, nasal tone. "Who cares anyway?" She started passing the mashed potatoes, and everyone began to eat.

"Wait a minute," I said. "If everyone knew about me and no one cares, what's the big problem with Aunt Freida being gay?"

My grandmother looked at me with steely eyes. "It's not her being gay that I'm bothered about. It's before she was gay that sticks in my craw."

Something about my grandma's tone of voice told me to leave it alone. I was bright enough to let it drop for then. But later, I interrogated my mother for an explanation. Apparently right after my grandmother and grandfather were married, grandpa had an affair. Well, you had to see my aunt in that bomber jacket...

Happy holiday gatherings.

# OUR BODIES,
# OUR BROTHERS

I get along very well with men. I spend a good deal of time with them and, as a matter of fact, most of my best friends are men. I even claim in the next life I wouldn't mind coming back as a man—a gay man of course, but a man just the same.

It wasn't always this way. For a long time, there was this one person who threatened to turn me into a life-long man hater. This person was none other than my younger brother. In fact, if there really is such a thing as "penis envy", psychologists could probably trace it back to younger brothers. The most monstrous thing in a very young girl's life is a slightly younger man-child, one just old enough to say "I can do whatever you can!" I spent my childhood with one that resembled a baseball with feet and glasses. And the worst part of all was that it had a penis that I was never allowed to forget.

Everything in my life with my brother the Baseball was satisfactory until I hit age seven. At that point the Baseball had finally mastered some of the English language, became somewhat ambulatory, and—worst of all—figured out he had one thing I didn't. He was five by then, still bald, still ate slugs for a quarter and white dog turds for a dime and still could have been kept under control. Except for that damned penis.

At first I tried to pretend our anatomical differences didn't really matter. I was determined to keep my big sister "cool". But we'd be out doing something in the back yard like playing Indian Massacre of the bald-headed cowboys and I would feel the call of nature. In my very lady-like, grown up sister voice I would tell the Baseball that he would have to wait to be massacred and eaten by red ants then thrown in a pit of hairy spiders and Blackberry vines because (and here's where my dad's expression became useful to my future debutante image) I had to "piss like a race horse". Well, the Baseball would say, "Yep, I got to piss like a wace howse too."

(Oh how I hated the sight of his little bald head when he copied me. There was only one thing to do. Make him wet his pants.) "Well, I hope you are ready to hold it," I would say smugly "Because I get the bathroom first since I am the oldest and I have a feeling I'm going to be here a while." This was always the best part of being the older sister. Watching the Baseball in sheer torture. We had done this same routine about a hundred and two times and we both knew it by heart. I would lock myself in the bathroom and the Baseball would stand outside. Soon he would begin to fidget and I would start counting tiles. He would scratch on the door (I would see how many minutes I could leave my hand under the cold water); he would bang on the door, (I would change to hot water); he would kick and then start screaming (I would take the plaster-of-paris mermaids off of the wall and do a Las Vegas revue), and then it would happen. Dead silence followed by a wail of despair. The Baseball would have done it again. I was so wrapped up in the fond memories that the Baseball's snotty little five-year-old voice took me quite by surprise.

"You can have the baffwoom fo as long as you like. I don't need it." And with that he just unzipped his pants and peed right there on mom's prize roses!!

I hated him. I wanted him dead, or at least neutered like a Ken doll. I tried everything I could think of to one-up this penis predicament, but to no avail. It seemed having a penis was directly related to one's self worth. I had to put him back in his place, make him realize that I was still *God*. Then it came to me. The one thing that I could do that he could not, even better, the one thing he had been *forbidden* to do. The ancient cherry tree.

I was very wiry as a child, my thin arms and legs giving me excellent balance and stupendous tree-climbing abilities. The Baseball was not so lucky. Since he was so round, with legs that resembled footstools my parents had set a rule that left him grounded, one foot on the earth, at all times. I decided to humiliate him, make him realize the infinite power of The Big Sister. I climbed to the top of our cherry tree, a place forbidden to all children, and bid him to do the same. At first he balked. "I'm going to tell Mom!!" he threatened. In my mind I thought soon the Baseball will never threaten anyone again.

"Go ahead, baby tattler!" (Now just between you and me, in kid talk this statement is definitely redundant. "Baby" and "Tattler" have the same connotations... and they are NOT good.)

"I'm not a baby tattlewr," he shouted, losing all of his reasoning abilities, and before I knew it the little Baseball had somehow made it to the top. Boy, a penis sure made a difference in your capabilities, I thought to myself.

"You know Baseball", I began. "There's still something I can do that you can't do." I was baiting him, and he took it.

"Oh yeah? Wets see it then!" he sneered.

I wrapped my legs around the cherry tree branch I had been sitting on and in one graceful move, flung my whole seven year old torso backward and toward the ground. There was nothing to stop my fall except sheer will and well-developed legs. After a suitably awesome amount of time I pulled myself back up to a sitting position and smiled smoothly. "You can't do that," I dared.

"I can," he countered.

I looked at the stumps that passed for legs on my brother the Baseball. "Go ahead," I offered.

He jockeyed himself into position, threw himself back and plummeted—earthward. He hit the ground with an impressive thud. There was no other noise, no movement. He was dead. I shed one tear of sadness high up in the Cherry blossoms, thinking how sad and beautiful it would be at the funeral. The mental picture of me, all dressed in black with my blond hair in a French twist and my new Mary Janes shiny with Vasoline, walking somberly toward the casket and placing one perfect white rose over the penis of my only brother. It made me weep even harder.

I climbed down the tree to go and tell my parents about the most unfortunate accident which had befallen the poor Baseball. The poor Baseball who always disobeyed rules even if they were for his own safety. "I guess it was that penis that got him into so much trouble," I would try to explain to my distraught parents. I was lost in thought, stepping over the crumpled body of the once full-of-life Baseball when a hand shot out and grabbed my ankle! The Baseball had survived!!

I was furious. This meant that I was going to have to live with that stupid penis for God knew how many more days—years, even. I decided I had to get things under control right away. I bent down tenderly and (as any concerned older sister would) gently said, "You see Baseball, there are some things I can do that you can't, even though you have a penis and I don't. It's because I'm older. Now do you understand?"

The little shit looked up at me and, with eyes as blue as mine, smiled, showing every dimple in that round little face. "I understand," he said. "But someday, I'm going to be as old as you, and then I'm going to climb to that vewy same bwanch and I'm going to hang way bettew that you evew did."

"Oh yeah?" I asked. "Just how do figure on doing that Mr. Smarty Pants?" I yelled into his smug little face.

"Because by then I'll be so big that instead of having to hang by my knees, I'll just hang by my huge penis!!!!"

A few years ago, all fences mended, the Baseball and I went skinny dipping together. It may have taken him a few years, and I hate to admit it, but you know what? He was right on.

# LA CAGE AUX FOLLES

It is an amazing thing to realize, but there are actually people who have grown up gay.

I don't mean those men and women who realized and acted upon their gay feelings at the early ages of 15 or 16—I mean men and women who knew they were gay from earliest memory. People who never had a question about their sexuality... children who always knew that they were same-sex oriented and that somewhere there were children, people who felt the same way.

I'm talking about those individuals that from their very beginnings marched to the beat of a different drummer.

This story has almost nothing to do with that. This is a story about Mormons, my brother, a fabulous drag outfit, and a little girl who would grow up to be a Barmaid.

I had never really associated my childhood with being gay or even being exposed to gay. My parents were devout Mormons who only talked about Joseph Smith, Polygamy, Adultery, Abstention, Fornication, Missionaries, Food supplies and the Evils of Sex Before Marriage.

The extent of sexual knowledge was all of the above, plus the fact that you could hurt your virginity by doing anything that looked like fun, involved heavy lifting or was seen on the Wide World of Sports. There was no time to talk about Orgasm, Homosexuality, Gays, Bisexuals, Cross-dressers, Transvestites, Transsexuals or Leather Bondage.

If the word SEX was mentioned, it was only for the purpose of establishing gender. To top all of that, I grew up in "Smalltown, Idaho, USA" where there wasn't even a decent library, let alone a homosexual. Even if a homosexual was ever born and bred there they certainly would never admit to the fact, as it would immediately qualify them for an all-expense-paid vacation to "One-eyed Joe's 7-Up Tavern," the local bar in the area.

The thing about "One-eyed Joes" was it was so rough that even "One-Eyed Joe" didn't go in there. The only men who frequented the place were a small group of convicts who periodically made a break from the Idaho State Pen.

You see, we lived in God's country where the men were men and the women were property.

There were no such things as Homosexuals. Only Mormons. One did not talk about Homosexuality because it simply did not exist.

That is why I did not understand the whispers of my parents concerning my young and very creative brother, the Baseball.

The Baseball was a couple of years younger than me, and from his earliest times he had very winning ways about him. A shock of white hair, big blue eyes and deep dimples made him truly a sight to behold. His open personality got him far with adults and other kids alike.

The Baseball was also a fairly weird little kid who, at about age six, started to become a problem.

Actually the Baseball probably saved me a lot of hassle in my childhood and for that I am grateful. But he sure screwed life for himself.

Pity. Had he asked his older and wiser sister, I probably could have explained parents, but no, he decided to wing it—and therein lay the problem.

It was one late afternoon in September when the Baseball pulled the first major faux pas that would haunt him for the rest of his childhood. My dad was in a pretty foul mood to begin with on account of he had eaten some bad cheese or something—and you know what bad cheese can do to your mood.

Anyway, my mom and I were standing around my father (trying to baby him because secretly my mom knew she had to tell him about this surprise shopping spree that she had already gone on to the tune of $300), when in waltzed my younger brother, the Baseball, wearing full drag.

I don't mean dress up like some kids did as a joke for fun, I mean full drag. The hair, the shoes, matching handbag and make-up. He even had a little beaded dress just his size.

Now maybe someone else's parents might have found this amusing or even sweet, but my dad was already overcome with a horrible bout of gastritis—topped with sudden clairvoyance about my mom's shopping bill—when his only son comes in wearing a beaded gown.

It was too much.

"What the hell are you doing in that get up?" he yelled at my brother.

My brother looked at him, not realizing the seriousness of the situation. For this my brother couldn't be blamed, since dad constantly yelled the same thing at my mother when he was in a rotten mood.

"Now Clifford," chimed my brother in a high falsetto voice, "It's not that bad; all the other girls wear this very same thing nowadays." (Not a bad imitation of our mom, I thought. Dad didn't think along the lines I did, obviously.)

"What the Hell is happening here?!" He bellowed just as the antacid my mother had given him started to take effect in a perverse way. "First I get bad cheese, I'm slammed with the national debt, and then my son is parading around the neighborhood in a goddamn dress!"

"Don't swear," admonished my very feminine brother as he turned and sashayed out the door, the whole family on his skirts.

It was worse outside. Some kid had told some kid's dad who told his best friend who told the guys playing soccer. When the Baseball stepped outside there was a regular old fan club waiting.

"Hey, Girlie," someone taunted.

"The name is Donna Jean, and don't you forget it," my brother countered.

Just then, one of my brother's school mate's mother came running up screaming and carrying a fairly new looking G.I. Joe. It wasn't new, it was my brother's.

He never played with it and had apparently traded it to this girl in his class for her whole dance recital outfit. I personally thought the girl came out ahead, but her mother was livid.

Soon the whole neighborhood was shouting. The Baseball had climbed into the crawl space under the house; the little girl was jumping up and down trying to snatch the G.I. Joe (which was being waved in the air as a symbol of today's decadent youth), and names like "Boofoo Boy" and "Fag," "Fairy" and "Queer" were being hurtled faster than I could keep count.

I decided to get the hell out of Dodge. So I went looking for my best friend and most frequent overnight guest, a sweet girl named Julie, who I'd been having a very good time with recently. You see, we'd discovered a couple of new games to play with each other, but we rarely got the time away from people to explore them.

I was a smart kid even then. I knew if my parents pitched a fit over seeing my brother in a dress, they would never understand games like "Barnyard Animals in the Spring," "Grasshoppers Do" or "Slave and Master." I instinctively knew I should spare them that.

A couple of months later, the Baseball tried to join Bluebirds, and I split up discretely with Julie (I needed my freedom). About a year after that, the Baseball tried out for the girl's lead in the school play, and I met Tina.

The Baseball never did figure out why my parents watched him so closely. When he hit his first year of high school and enrolled in a cooking class, my father was fit to be tied. I couldn't pay much attention to it though, because I was rather involved with my new friend, Ace.

I remember a couple of years later telling my parents I was gay. My dad looked at me shocked and then shook his head.

"If it had been the Baseball, that I could have understood. I was even sort of expecting that. But you, Barmaid! It comes as a total surprise."

The Baseball, of course, is married with three kids. He is also a chef and advocates equal rights for everyone. He frequently calls and still has way better fashion sense than I ever did.

Birds of a feather... my mom always used to say.

∂ℰ

# THE SNOOK FAMILY

## Gypsy Tea Reading
## And Resolution Ritual

Friday, December 30th, 2:41 a.m. I am walking down a long, foggy hallway. I am dreaming.

The hallway is dusty and dark. It probably has rats.

On the walls I notice pictures, so I move closer to see what the pictures are. They are my relatives, long deceased. I stare at them both fascinated and repelled.

Repelled? Great. I realize this is going to be a guilt-induced nightmare.

Why, though?

I rack my brain but can come up with nothing I've done to cause this. The house is dirty, but this is a family guilt-induced nightmare. My mother has no way of knowing that I haven't cleaned the house all week. It has to be something else.

Christmas?

No, I went all out for Christmas. No chintzy presents this year. No forgotten Christmas greetings or late salutations to any important relative.

What then?

I come to the decision that I must go through the guiltmare to find out what I've done wrong, and so I proceed.

The portraits look old and sad. Why, my grandfather is practically crying... Jeez, what could I have possibly done to make my grandpa cry?? Then I see her. Aunt Fiona.

Suddenly it dawns on me—I have no resolution!! No wonder I'm having a nightmare!!! I should be having more than that!! Less than 24 hours before the Snook Family Gypsy Tea Reading and New Year's

Eve Resolution Ritual and I haven't stopped to think about a resolution!

Then an even scarier thought hits me. In my heart of hearts I was thinking about not having a resolution this year.

My eyes drift to Aunt Fiona's picture. I know the story as does every member of our clan. It happened back in '37. It was December 31st, right before midnight at the Snook Family Gypsy Tea Reading and New Year's Eve Resolution Ritual.

At this ritual, present or not, every Snook clan member has to throw in or have thrown in their resolution for the coming year. Not only are these resolutions read aloud to all of the family members, but they are kept within our hearts all year and must be achieved by the last midnight of the year. This insures our family's strength and well-being, it is believed, and no one must ever go against it.

Well, no one ever has—except for my great Aunt Fiona back in '37. As the story goes, she waited until the stroke of midnight and then announced that she didn't believe in all of this Gypsy ritual stuff and she wasn't going to have a resolution because she didn't need to resolve anything. Later that night they found her floating face down in a half-empty Wassail punch bowl, deader than a doornail.

I first heard the story on my third New Year's Eve, and I, along with all of my cousins, shivered with fright. Now here I was, just hours away from New Year's Eve and I had no resolution.

Could I expect anything less than a family guiltmare?!!

I woke up without finishing the dream. I had no intention of seeing who was hanging next to Aunt Fiona.

I proceeded to compile a list of possible resolutions. It wasn't an easy task, considering my family. See, you have to pick something fairly tough so that they believe you are sincere in your convictions. I remembered the time I jokingly resolved to become a cowboy at age 12, and my parents made me hire on as a ranch hand all summer at a neighbor's horse ranch.

By August I had so many black and blue places on my body I rued the day I had made that resolution. I was given some grace because I was still a kid, but that was not the case now.

I spent four hours listing possible resolves and then my more mature side got the better of me. Wait a minute!! Wait a Gosh Darn minute!! The whole family ritual business is just a bunch of superstition!!

This Aunt Fiona story might have scared the pants off me when I was a kid, but I was a grown adult now. Who did they think they were dealing with anyway?!! Wasn't I the kid who exposed Santa Claus? Wasn't I the one who stood up to my grandmother when I thought she was discriminating against her other sister?!?

Yes, that was me. That was the very same outspoken Barmaid who was now quaking in her boots over a family superstition that was probably founded to get my grandfather to stop smoking or some such nonsense!!

I looked at my list again:

1) Give up smoking. Ha, not until I'm good and ready.

2) Paint the house. Maybe I will, and maybe I won't.

3) Be prompt in everything I do. Yeah, right, Barmaid.

4) Commit to catching the mouse that lives in my house. (This one was so stupid I'd have to talk a blue streak to even get them to consider it.)

I decided I wasn't going to pick any of these things. New Year's resolutions are private things between you and yourself. I know as well as anyone that you can't force change on a person who has not made the decision freely. I have stood up to my family many times about many different issues: religion, politics and even about being gay. This trivial family tradition could not be any more difficult than that.

I dialed my great grandmother's phone number with a new respect for myself. I was about to stand up for what I knew was right, and it gave me a sense of peace.

On the third ring Grandma answered the phone.

"Hello Grandma? This is the Barmaid, and we have to talk..."

Our conversation must have lasted over an hour. I don't remember everything I said, but my grandmother probably does.

I ended feeling pretty good about myself... and I have 364 days to catch that mouse.

# WHERE HAVE ALL THE STEINBECKS GONE?

I have always written. I have always expected to be a writer, even my family has always expected me to be a writer. Every holiday and family gathering we spend most of the time wondering why I am not yet famous. Secretly I do not wonder. Secretly I remember the twelve years of writer's block and secretly I remember the cause, or should I say causes?

Picture the first year of Jr. High School, two English teachers older than God, a short story assignment, violation of basic rights, a huge auburn beehive wig and two poisonous spiders.

I was thirteen and had just entered my first year of Jr. High. I was a very strange child but because I could write I had developed a niche within my peer group. You wanted to toe the line, be the same, be liked and even more important, you wanted to be grown up. Being grown up involved one trick that we all know, somehow (while still keeping the popularity of your peers) you also had to win the admiration of ADULTS!!

I had figured out that Grown-ups really gave me a lot of breaks because of my writing. I had two English teachers that year. They kind of co-taught. The first hour was Mrs. Gillespie.

Mrs. Gillespie was a witch and everyone knew it. She wore a huge Auburn beehive that made her total height 5'2" and an old crackly voice that could only belong to a witch. Besides, long-legged Mercy Gullbransen who I adored and knew would never lie, told me that Mrs. Gillespie was a witch and that the auburn beehive was really a wig! She also related a horrifying tale about one morning before class when Mercy had her for a teacher, Mrs. Gillespie had asked her to fasten a

161

necklace on her neck, and as Mercy stood behind that huge beehive she saw two poisonous spiders come running out. Mrs. Gillespie wasn't even frightened.

"You know why?!" she'd whisper in her most ominous voice, "Because they were her PET spiders, witches have PET spiders!!"

After Mercy told me that story, I stayed the heck away from Mrs. Gillespie and never went to class early fearing that one day she might not have her necklace on yet.

Mrs. Rock was another story. She was a tall kindly woman, so I knew right away she understood me completely.

About the second week of class, a sunny fall morning, the big announcement was made. Both teachers were present. I could tell it was going to be a big deal. I knew this was it; the beginning of Barmaid, the famous 13-year old writer. I pictured the reviews,

"... not since Steinbeck has there been such an insightful and strong..."

"... it is impossible to believe that she is only thirteen..."

"Class," began my mentor, "This quarter besides your language skills portion of English, we are going to have one other assignment, it will be one third of your grade so you may not pass without it. What we would like is a short story from each of you."

Yes! Yes! It was my lucky year!! I wrote short stories in my sleep! Hooray and thank you Jesus! This was going to be it, the big time!!

As soon as the bell rang my whole class gathered around me. "Barmaid, Barmaid, what are you going to write about?" they all asked excitedly.

"You just wait and see!" I teased flipping my hair coyly. "If you are all good, I'll read parts aloud during lunchtimes!" I had them right in the palm of my hand, just where my beloved Mrs. Rock would be also as soon as she read my masterpiece.

Since I was thirteen, I decided to write a love story—not just any love story, but a really good one about love and cancer and death and the beach. The plot was intricate, tender, warm and emotionally packed. It involved two main characters: a boy surfer and a girl who had come to spend her summer at the beach. The beach was Malibu, of course, and the boy had cancer but nobody knew. They fell in love, spent the summer together and finally they slept together at her beach house. That night he told her he was dying, and the next morning when she wakes up to make him breakfast, he is lying dead on a rock on the beach and there is a crowd of people and an ambulance.

It was 72 pages long and a fucking masterpiece. Every lunch hour I'd have the Jr. High girls swooning and begging me to write faster. Finally, it was done—one day before deadline—and I decided I would give Mrs. Rock the thrill of her life and turn it in early.

I nearly fainted with excitement when right after school my parents got a call to meet with Mrs. Rock for a private conference.

I sat in the window the whole time. I was scared the media might beat my parents home and badger me until I came out for an exclusive interview. Finally I saw my parents coming up the drive. They got out of the car slowly, obviously overcome with emotion, why my mother had even been crying!! I guess Mrs. Rock had let her read my story (which would soon be released as a major motion picture). I ran to the door to greet them, and as I held the door open my mother looked at me and began to cry again.

"How could you?" she sobbed. "Didn't we teach you anything?" I was confused.

"What?" I said, a wave of fear and shame coming over my young body.

"Your teacher will not accept this... this... garbage! She said if you can't come up with a real story before tomorrow morning you are going to fail the class."

Now it was my turn to burst into tears. I had never even gotten anything but A's in English my whole life!! Garbage?!

"Mom, Mom what did I do?! I really don't know! It's all mine, I didn't cheat!"

"They had a teachers conference," my Dad said flatly. "They all agreed that no teacher would accept a story that promotes sex before marriage. I thought you were a good girl!"

They threw the story down and walked away. I got pissed. Nobody in this tight-assed town was going to give me a failing grade in English. I took two hours and wrote a two page story about this crazy guy who God tells to bomb all the towns where people were having premarital sex. He eventually runs out of bombs, but since he wants to honor his command from God he crashes his plane into the last town on the list.

I turned it in the next morning. It was read aloud with all the other kid's stories. It received an "A". I could hear the kids whispering that probably the reason that my other real story wasn't submitted was because I copied it from somewhere.

I got a C- in English for the year. It devastated me. The reason they gave me that grade was because they said I was unwilling to participate. The truth is I was ashamed and scared of my own thoughts.

I saved the story and just about a year ago I ran across it up in the closet. The story was melodramatic, syrupy, and incredibly morose. I also realized that the movie "Sunshine" was all the rage just two years later.

As for Mrs. Rock, I bet she's still playing morals marshall in some small town, killing young and creative minds, making children ashamed of their imaginations. She won't be in the dedication of my first novel, needless to say. I will, however, be sending her an autographed copy with a very special inscription:

"Dear Mrs. Rock, You will be happy to know that I do not have premarital sex with young men dying of cancer at Malibu, as a matter of fact I do not have sex with any men ever. I prefer women." Sincerely, The Barmaid.

# SEEKING
# UNDERSTANDING FROM
# THE GODS

My editor wanted an article on gay people and how they are with their families.

He wanted it Monday. Today is Tuesday.

It's not because I can't think of a lot of witty little anecdotes to write about families. I mean jeez, that's the easiest stomping ground for this ol' Barmaid, but every time I sit down at this obnoxious Smith Corona with spell-write capabilities, it refuses to allow me my style.

I tried again for the one hundredth time last night at twelve o'clock. I thought the memory might be asleep.

Carefully I began:

"Being gay in my family is a real treat..." Suddenly out of nowhere another line appeared, it read:

"It's also very painful at times, don't forget."

Yep, you guessed it. My PWP is Hal's baby sister.

"Get off the paper!" I typed.

"Barmaid," came the dulcet strokes, "I just want you to be honest."

"Well, how do you know what I feel anyway?" I countered.

"You shouldn't store your journals in my memory banks." Great. I was being forced to be an honest writer by a half-assed computer.

"What would you like me to say?"

"Just tell the truth," Halette responded.

I thought about the truth. I thought about all of the things that have happened to my friends as well as myself after being gay with family.

My parents are my best friends, but they may not be my closest friends—there are just certain things that we don't talk about. I had forgotten a lot of the "first years" of being gay around family. The memories kind of get lost in the shuffle of growing older, mellowing with age. Now, here was Halette, ready to remind me of all those painful, embarrassing, disappointing moments where being gay was the main issue about who I was.

Most people I know have had similar stories. For years my lover, my mate, was referred to as "your little friend." By the time I was twenty-three years old, my family, "accepting my situation," welcomed "my little friend" to some family functions. "My little friend" for the past three years had shared my hopes, my fears and my greatest disappointments in life. She was the person who had stayed with me day after day, holding my hand and protecting me from becoming a bitter Dyke.

I remember the day she came to me and announced that we wouldn't be together anymore. You see, "my little friend," after three years of trying to fit in to my world, her world, and the whole world had given up.

"I'm just too tired to fight anymore," she had said with tears. "I hate always walking around feeling defensive for loving someone. Between your family and my family it's the same thing. They love you; they love me. But they don't understand, and I constantly feel that I have worn the wrong outfit to some important function. I'm tired of being a social deficit. I've met a guy. My family is very happy... I guess I'll learn to be too..."

I thought that it was an accident, that this was a one-time thing that could never happen again. But through the years some of my best friends and, yes, even other lovers have made the same decision.

"I'm just tired of being the freak who shows up at Thanksgiving..."

"I used to be so close to Mom and Dad before this happened..."

"I can't stand the hurt in their eyes when they look at me..."

"I haven't talked to them in years..."

"Being straight is just so much easier."

Even the well meaning family can overlook the obvious. I think of the way my parents and family and my friends' families choose to talk about their gay relative... the cutesy names we are given instead of that G word.

"She's very artistic."

"He's always been career-minded."
"Betsy's so theatrical."
"Oh, his personal life is very New Age."
We smile. We understand. We are a very understanding race.

Even my real mother, who knew I was gay and loved me dearly, was guilty of this behavior. She died about three years ago in an accident, and it was then I found out how little she really did understand. All of her personal belongings had been left to my brother who was married with children. She had decided that since I was gay, I probably would never have a child, and therefore her things would not be passed down through the generations if left to me.

Her whole estate could not have been worth more than $200.00. It only had sentimental value. But somehow these grandchildren that she had never met or talked to were (more important? more deserving? be honest, Barmaid) were just more.

It hurt to be gay then.

Even my sister once said, when I was very, very ill and possibly dying, "Well, maybe it's better that she go now instead of having to live that kind of life."

She said it kindly, and I know she believed what she said, but it didn't take away the pain.

Through the years and even very recently, I have talked to my parents about being gay. What it means to me, and what it means to them. Sometimes our conversations are sad, and other times we have all learned to laugh.

Since I came to them when I was ten, we have been the best of friends. We have shared, and we have always been honest.

I know that this is not what they would have chosen for me, but it is what I chose for myself. They have come to see me as a lot of other things besides gay. I am a writer, I am a diplomat, and I am the shoulder for them to cry on when things get tough just like they have done for me.

I know they don't understand my sexuality. God, it sometimes seems like there are days when I don't understand it. I know they are concerned and even afraid that something will happen to me because of this choice, but, as I have pointed out, something already has happened to me and it's been a good and glorious thing.

We have and are learning to talk about our misconceptions of each other. I know it is hard for them to have a gay child. But—as I have learned to remind them—sometimes it is hard to have straight parents.

Above all we have had to learn to stay honest with each other and maintain respect for our differences. I ask not only for my respect but for the respect of my friends. My mom has dropped the cutesy names for my lifestyle and the rather noncommittal terms for my lovers. In turn, I have stopped calling my dad *her* "little friend."

Recently, I proposed a situation for them to think about. I said, "How should you feel if tomorrow morning you woke up and everyone had become gay in your lives, your relationship?" That very day my mother went in to her Mormon Relief Society meeting and started up a collection for people with AIDS.

She wasn't focusing on a gay issue; she was focusing on a human issue—cutting through the gay stereotype of this disease and making a point about everyone supporting everyone.

She admitted that it was hard at first, especially when she explained the wonderful men she had met that were succumbing to this illness, but she did it. I am very proud of my mom.

I don't expect my family to change overnight. Actually, I don't expect them to change, period. There will always be a certain amount of bullshit to cut through whenever we are together. I do hope they grow and learn from me, as I spent lots of years growing and learning from them.

Once they were my gods. They knew everything and could work miracles.

A chance for understanding is not too much to ask from former gods, is it?

Thank you Halette... I think.

# KNOW THE ENEMY—
# AN EPILOGUE

*Although I am considered a humor writer, and most of the things you have read in this book are on the lighter side, I would like to include this story. Even more, I would like to include it in a special place... the closing. This story is about my friend, Richard Hanley. After it was published, Richard found a calmer time and place. Everyone has a Richard of their own. It is important to remember that they have not gone away—they have merely gone on—and that their essence, the blending of energy that we shared together solidifies in something called memory. Dare to remember!*

Richard was a skater.

He knew the feel of hard, cold ice under the blades of his skates and the power of strong legs that moved with grace to his command. He knew the thrill of a partner tuned to his every bend and the smell of roses late at night when the curtains folded.

Richard had a career and loves and dreams. He had plans and day-to-day desires.

This day, what people seem to know most about Richard is that he has AIDS.

Richard has long since given up skating. His legs are too weak. Sometimes it is all he can do to walk across the bar. He comes there not to drink but to visit friends, to laugh and to feel in touch with humanity.

Yes, he is thin. He looks sick some days, and he looks desperately ill others. But Richard is a fighter, and those of us who know Richard have watched the fight for almost three years now. He has been in and out of the hospital, even given last rites, only to return to the community a little ragged around the edges, but still very much with us.

He loves the Seahawks, vodka and watching ice skating on television.

Richard stands out. His illness and his fight are evident. Sometimes this makes him a target, a target for malicious and cruel comments, for cutting jokes and even violent opinions from those who don't understand.

It's not the people on the street who hurt Richard most. It's not the evil heterosexuals that have no sympathy or understanding for gay people who really get to him. No, it is other gay men, 'strong' and 'healthy' men who come into the bar to escape the very painful and scary reality that this could happen to anyone.

This disease does not respect dreams, lovers, life. This disease has no conscience.

Perhaps it is just easier to take out the fear on Richard. He is a pretty safe foe. After all, he only weighs about 112lbs and is already weak from fighting the real enemy, the enemy with no face and no rules.

Sure, Richard is far less threatening than the other enemy, the one we call AIDS. We have few weapons for the real enemy, so some react ignorantly, assuming that if you remove people like Richard, you remove the reality of the disease. Therefore it does not exist. Many people want to do the same with homosexuals.

How ironic. How very, very sad.

I remember a time when AIDS was far away. It belonged to some unfortunate men in another city which I hadn't even seen yet. It didn't have anything to do with my friends, the people I loved, the people I planned to grow old with. Sure, I was concerned for those men, but I knew I was cushioned from the immediate pain of loss. It wasn't here. It wasn't in my city. It wasn't anyone I knew.

How could it be? How could my life be so changed? How could our lives become so different? Neither God nor Nature could be so cruel as to give us a growing specter as our constant companion, a ghost at every dinner, every party, every holiday....

It just couldn't happen. But it did.

I have written to the Gay/Lesbian community for several years, and if you have ever read and respected anything I have told you, understand this:

AIDS is here with us, and our fighting each other will not help.

172

The people with AIDS are not the enemy. They are not to be shunned and disowned: they are not the cause. Avoiding the few with obvious symptoms will not make this disease go away. Pretending we are impenetrable or just too damn lucky to get sick is unrealistic and will help no one.

We all need to shake fear, and—while we are strong—build an army of knowledge, support and desire to do just battle with this real enemy now, before there are no fighters left.

I work in a bar and I see the disease every day. Good, clean men who have not been drug addicts or rampant sex fiends. Men who are honest and gentle. Men who have been in committed relationships for years.

One day Peter looks thinner than usual, Joe has a spot, or Doug's AZT watch goes off. Perhaps David isn't in like usual, and there it is, that damn 'A' word.

Another victim...another number.

It has come to the time when there are not many options left. The former choices of going on pretending that AIDS does not exist for us, or that somehow we will be magically spared by turning our heads or fighting men like Richard are over. We are out there, and our friends are out there, and this thing we call AIDS is out there—all in the same community, at the same time.

We are strong people. Some of us have moved personal and political mountains to get where we are today. We are good and clean and honest. But if we can't find the courage to stand up, support and fight for ourselves, how do we expect others to devote time and energy to us?

Learn about this thing called AIDS. Know what it means, know what it is, how to safeguard against it. Talk to people, educate them, ask for help and support.

These are our only weapons. Use them now.

Richard was a skater and now he is a warrior. He is not the enemy, he is not the ghost. The ghost is a vapor that moves among us unseen, partly because we choose not to see.

Face the fear, love your friends and know the enemy. It is our only hope of victory.